Elections in the Middle East

About the Book and Editor

The far-reaching impact of the latest parliamentary elections in the Middle East is examined in this volume. After an introduction that analyzes the trends illustrated by the elections and their implications for regional stability, the book discusses recent elections in Turkey, Egypt, Israel, Jordan, and Kuwait. Individual chapters analyze the influence of pre-1980 patterns in the party system and voting on Turkey's 1983 election; the balloting in Egypt's 1984 election as a turning point toward democratization in contemporary Egyptian politics; the significance of Israel's 1984 election in view of the relatively small differences in objectives between Israel's right wing Likud and the centrist Labor party; the role of traditional tribal influences and new political factions in Jordan's 1984 elections; and the influence of newly emerging social groups in Kuwait's 1985 election. The contributors discuss differences in party programs and platforms, the extent of control by elites, and the relevance of the elections to crucial economic and social problems and political stability.

Linda L. Layne is a lecturer in anthropology at Princeton University.

Elections in the Middle East
Implications of Recent Trends

edited by Linda L. Layne

Westview Press / Boulder and London

Westview Special Studies on the Middle East

This Westview softcover edition is printed on acid-free paper and bound in
softcovers that carry the highest rating of the National Association of State
Textbook Administrators, in consultation with the Association of American Pub-
lishers and the Book Manufacturers' Institute.

Published in 1987 in the United States of America by Westview Press, Inc;
Frederick A. Praeger, Publisher; 5500 Central Avenue, Boulder, Colorado 80301

Library of Congress Catalog Card Number: 85-51183
ISBN: 0-8133-0298-6

Composition for this book was provided by the editor.
This book was produced without formal editing by the publisher.

Printed and bound in the United States of America

The paper used in this publication meets the requirements of the
American National Standard for Permanence of Paper for Printed
Library Materials Z39.48-1984.

6   5   4   3   2   1

CONTENTS

TABLES AND FIGURES

ix

PREFACE

The chapters on Egypt, Israel, Jordan, and Turkey were first presented as part of a session "Recent Middle East Elections: Implications for Instability" organized by Don Peretz and held at the Eighteenth Annual Meeting of the Middle East Studies Association, San Francisco, November 28th through December 1st, 1984. The chapter on Kuwait was added later.

The chapters vary in emphasis and approach. Each was written independently and the authors are trained in a number of different fields (anthropology, sociology and politics). Three of the chapters (Egypt, Jordan and Kuwait) were written by anthropologists. As a result, they not only seek to interpret the elections per se, but use the elections as vehicles with which to attain a greater understanding of the workings of the culture and society as a whole. Although neither Moench nor Gavrielides were able to observe first-hand the elections about which they write, their in-depth knowledge of Egypt and Kuwait affects the type of questions each asks and adds richness to their interpretations. Because elections generate large amounts of quantitative data, electoral behavior is assumed to be particularly amenable to comparative analysis. While such statistical comparisons between nations can be hazardous, ridden as they are by exclusion of un-quantifiable social and cultural differences, Erguder and Hofferbert make excellent use of statistical materials to study difference within Turkey.

I am indebted to Don Peretz for the opportunity to edit this volume. I would also like to thank the authors for their cooperation and patience and to express my gratitude to Beth Shally, Mary Taylor Huber and Bernard Wilson for their assistance.

L.L.L.

Chapter I

INTRODUCTION

Linda L. Layne

Of the institutions of democratic states, elections are among the most prominent in manifesting political participation and bringing about or legitimating change in political regimes. It is elections that give political leaders the most direct and obvious incentive to take note of the wishes and views of ordinary people. This book discusses the elections which took place in 1983, 1984, and 1985 in five Middle Eastern countries. These papers do more than simply report election results. In addition to interpreting the outcomes of these particular elections, the contributors seek to understand the meaning of the electoral systems within these societies. While each of the five electoral systems described in this book resemble those of the west, each has developed and been affected by local traditions. Many of these essays challenge familiar assumptions based on western experience and question the appropriateness of western political models when seeking to understand the elections of Middle Eastern nations. Those interested in explaining the outcomes of elections, ascertaining the content of any mandates issued to winning candidates, gauging the decisiveness of victory or defeat, and assessing the type of judgments that enter into voting, must take into account the particularities of the history and development of each electoral system and the structure and culture of the societies of which they are a part. In addition to the laws and mechanisms of voting, the character, attitudes and behavior of the voters and the elected in each society vary. The problems facing these states

1

varies, and these differences find expression in the electoral laws and campaigns and in the composition and character of the elected assemblies.[1] Efforts to understand why formally similar political institutions perform differently in different societies inevitably leads one away from a strictly political focus to consideration of the wider aspects of each society.

Democratic elections and parliamentary systems are fundamental elements of representational government. But what exactly is being represented? Elections not only express the will of the people concerning particular policies and issues, but also ideas about the collectivity as such, conceptions of the nature and function of the state, the parameters of legitimate political behavior for candidates, leaders, and citizens,[2] the requirements of authority and leadership, people's conceptions of themselves as belonging to the imagined community of the nation-state, and what they expect from the governing body of that state.[3]

The belief that elections carry obvious messages is widely shared in democratic nations and has been a premise of many democratic theorists. For example, John Stuart Mill saw elections as a "periodical muster of opposing forces, to gauge the state of the national mind, and ascertain, beyond dispute, the relative strength of different parties and opinions" (1962:230). However, elections patently fall within what Braudel calls "l'histoire evenementielle", the history of events. This type of history, according to Braudel, is ultra-sensitive by definition and by nature exciting and rich in human interest, but he cautions, it is also the most perilous, capricious, and delusive (Braudel 1980:3-4). Although elections, like other events encompassed by Braudel's term, take place in an instant, they are manifestations of larger and long-term forces and can only be fully understood in this context. The problems entailed in accurately interpreting what voters express when they vote has become increasingly recognized. Votes are now recognized as only an avowal of support at a particular time, and very often of support with reservations. A count of votes tells no one how far voters will follow the victorious candidate, or for how long, or in what direction and these uncertainties are compounded in systems with an electoral college such as in the USA or a district system as in Egypt.

Even landslides often give a quite misleading sense of the support that candidates enjoy. A large plurality may be the result of a freakish turnout, weak commitment of voters to the winning candidates, an unpopular victor (few people liked either candidate), or issues that were transient (Kelley 1983).[4] Moench (this volume) was confronted by the problems of assessing the strength of a mandate even after a strong electoral showing of support.

Those who do not vote are often as important as those who do. Arabs in Israel, Turkey's anti-system segment, and the majority of Egypt's urbanites all express important messages with their silence. In Egypt's 1985 election, although rural percentages were high, in urban areas barely one fifth of the registered voters turned out despite the threat of punishment. Of the non-participants, those who do not vote from an Islamic conviction that the secular state and its political process must be replaced by an Islamic society represent a special threat. In Israel voter participation increased in 1984 to 72% compared with 70% in 1981 according to government reports. Peretz and Smooha attribute this increase to Arabs who had boycotted elections in the past but voted in 1984 thanks to the Progressive List's peace option.

Election analysts now understand that in order to assess the decisiveness of any given election one needs to be able to answer the following questions. How fully did each side mobilize its adherents? For how many voters was the choice between candidates a close question? To what extent did the winning candidate's victory depend on the votes of such weakly committed voters? How favorable were the attitudes of individual voters toward the winning candidate? Did many see the person they support only as the lesser of two evils? Were the issues that contributed most to the outcome transient or enduring? If the latter, were the positions that the parties assumed

on such issues likely to become identified as partisan? (Kelley 1983:29). Campaign issues are also
often misleading, not necessarily identical with
latent, often broader national issues, which are
at stake.

Factors such as the age and size of the population, cultural homogeneity, and literacy levels
affect the meanings and outcomes of elections not
only in different nations, but also within the
same nations through time, thus affecting interpretations within a single country from one
election to the next. The importance of demographic changes, especially the percentage of
youthful population and related percentage of educated population, is a recurrent theme in the following analyses. For example, in Jordan the in-
clusion of women and the increasingly large
proportion of younger voters in the electorate including the first-time voters ages twenty to thir-
ty-seven made for a significantly changed electorate in 1985 from that which participated in
Jordan's last national elections held seventeen
years before. Orent (1985) argues that the
strength of a new civil religion "New Zionism"
which is replacing labor Zionism as Israel's dominant ideology is due, in large part, to the demographic rise and political maturation of Oriental
Jewry.

Each of the elections described in this collection was, for various reasons, the object of
special interest. Both the Jordanian and Turkish
elections discussed here took place after a period
of suspension and were, therefore, the object of
even greater than usual interest. The parliamentary by-elections which took place in Jordan in
1984 were the first national elections held since
1967. The restoration of democracy in Turkey and
the return to civil rule which the 1983 parliamentary elections marked, took place after Turkey's
longest period of military rule. Those interested
in Kuwait's political history found the 1985
elections fascinating as the effects of the 1981
redistricting continued to be played out while political groups adjusted their strategies to the
new system. This election, the second since the
five-year suspension of parliament in 1976, occured in the context of continuing uncertainty

generated by the Iraq-Iran war and the related concern about the strength and loyalty of the Islamic fundamentalists in Kuwait, as well as the dissatisfaction of the middle classes following the stock market collapse.[5] The holding of elections under these circumstances seemed a positive sign of the strength of democracy in Kuwait and the subsequent suspension of parliament proved a disappointment for many observers. Egypt's 1984 election was the first to be held under President Mubarak. Because Mubarak's political philosophy and leadership style were unknown and the strength of his support unclear, these elections were carefully watched both in and outside of Egypt.[6] There is a widespread feeling that an important shift is taking place within Israeli politics. The results of the eleventh Knesset election are, perhaps, the most important data on which observers of Israeli's political culture base their various interpretations. For example, Orent (1985) and Aronoff (1985) use the results from the 1984 election to argue their very different views concerning the current direction of Israeli politics.

Elections and Political Culture

We are not the first to recognize the importance of civil rituals such as elections in articulating important themes of a culture. Cohen's (1965) account of the 1959 general election and several simultaneous municipal elections in Arab villages in Israel focuses on the role of village social organization. In a setting where no country-wide Arab political organizations or parties existed, *hamulas* (clans) had important political functions. However, while the local council elections were fought mostly on *hamula* lines, *hamulas* played little role in the general Knesset elections. Given the lack of alternative Arab political organizations, many Israeli parties tried to exploit *hamula* groupings and cleavages on the assumption that if a *hamula* leader was won over he would automatically bring with him the votes of his *hamula* members (1965:154).[7] Cohen does not contest this assumption but argues that *hamula* leadership decided there was no reason for impos-

ing a unified policy on an issue which did not
touch the *hamula* as a group; each individual could
vote in accordance with his or her individual interests and circumstances. Men from the same *hamula* supported different parties and men from different and sometimes hostile *hamulas* supported the
same electoral lists. But at the village level,
where village autonomy was at risk, and where victory provided important connections to outside
sources of power and economic privileges for members of the village council and their supporters,
hamulas functioned as political parties, competing
with other *hamulas* for power and prestige (Cohen
1965:171).[8]

Rosen (1972 and 1984) has analysed the 1966
election of a representative to the Chamber of Agriculture in a rural constituency of central Morocco and the 1963 Moroccan parliamentary
elections. His study of these elections not only
adds to our understanding of the ongoing development of such political institutions, but also
highlights the nature of local and national political relations, as well as illuminating underlying
forces and processes which serve to energize and
typify a given society. Rosen showed how dis-
tinctly Moroccan means were often used by candidates to gain victory. The quest for political
supporters in this election was, he suggests, a
specific form of the more general and ongoing process of seeking social dependents and supporters.
Inherent in this process is the tendency to avoid
issues or practices that might hinder one's ability to choose associates from any part of the total
society for whatever situation might arise. In
fact, the reason people have avoided firm partisan
attachments holds also for kin-based loyalty.

Eickelman has demonstrated how even in instances where elections are not "free", the forms
of government intervention may tell us a great
deal about important social and political trends.
His (1986) analysis of changes in the form and
content of Morocco's elections since 1960 focuses
on the changing forms of government intervention
as a means of assessing long-term political shifts
in Morocco. Eickelman shows how since the
mid-1970s the patronage system of local notables,
while still important, is no longer the only sys-

tem operating in the rural areas. He links the progressive politicization of Morocco's smaller urban centers and a growing disenchantment with traditional vehicles of political expression with demographic changes, especially the growing size and sophistication of educated, politically active populations under thirty years of age (1986:193). Meeker (1972) has also focused on transformations of political culture. He explored the changing role of Turkish aghas, their techniques and styles of leadership in three historical contexts--in Ottoman society, under one-party rule, and under the present multi-party system.

Herzfeld's 1985 account of a municipal (1975) and parliamentary election (1977) in Greece provides an excellent case study of the ways that elections may express many levels of identity, a theme I develop in Chapter 5 of this volume.[9] Herzfeld highlights the performative aspects of electoral behavior. Each villager's electoral choices were acts of assertion of both individual and collective identity encapsulating allusions to many levels of social identity at one and the same time. His study, like Cohen's, points to the variable importance of kin-based solidarity in different electoral settings, or at least the extent to which these allegiances are foregrounded or downplayed in local assessments of the guiding principles of conduct for national and municipal elections (1985:111).

Volatility, Fragmentation, and Polarization of Party Systems (Turkey, Israel, and Egypt)

The social and ideological divisions revealed in elections can be used to characterize different political systems, including party systems. The concepts of volatility, fragmentation, and polarization which Erguder and Hofferbert identify as three maladies of the Turkish party system are also useful in discussing the party systems of Israel and Egypt.[10] Fragmentation refers to the number and internal discipline of parties. Volatility refers to the ability to predict bases of support and party fortunes for particular parties in one election from their performance in the preceeding contest. Polarization assesses the relative strength of the ideological poles and other dimensions over which the society is divided.

In both Turkey and Israel a parliamentary majority is deemed crucial to a stable government, but both suffer from the lack. Following a thirty year period (1920-1950) of one party rule in Turkey, fragmentation developed and grew steadily during the 1960s. No party was able to return a governing majority to the Turkish National Assembly in the elections of 1973 and 1977. The intense party competition of the 1970s led to parliamentary and governmental immobility and, according to Erguder and Hofferbert, thereby threatened both the contemporary function of the State as a modernizing agent and the perceived traditional role of the "State" as the cement of Turkish society which inturn led to the subsequent military intervention.

Although Turkey appears to be a classic two-party system of "moderate pluralism" with alternating coalition governments, center-oriented, with support for ideological poles being weak in terms of both electoral support and parliamentary representation, closer examination reveals it to be highly polarized--characterized by ideological intransigence, intolerance of criticism, and lack of accommodation between key actors.

Fragmentation is also a problem in Israel. Although Israel continues to be dominated by two parties, twenty-six parties competed in the 1984 elections, thirteen of which were new since the 1981 election. In addition to the number of parties, there was a great deal of intra-party squabbling over places on the electoral lists. Fragmentation was especially severe among religious parties, and among Arabs and the Left. Nevertheless, Peretz and Smooha see some good coming from fragmentation since it leads to coalitions in which both major blocks must address issues and consider solutions in a manner which might not otherwise be possible.

There is less polarization in Israel than in Turkey as both sides move towards the center. However, polarization is becoming increasingly defined along ethnic lines.[11] There has also been

less volatility in Israel than Turkey. Although
there have been changes in the political currents,
they tend to be fairly steady and constant, such
as an increasing conservative and nationalist sentiment among Israel's Jewish population, a small
but constant decrease in Oriental votes for Labor,
and Labor's ideological move towards the center.

Unlike Israel and Turkey, Egypt did return a
majority, with a substantial victory for the government's National Democratic Party. Fragmentation was relatively limited with only five parties
participating: two parties of the Left, two of the
Liberal Right, and the government party. According to Moench, none of the five represented a radical political position. The opposition was fragmented and hampered by a high level of
in-fighting. Despite all this, Moench questions
the meaning of Mubarak's landslide and the stability of his regime. Moench singles out the Islamic
fundamentalists as an important and unmeasured political element not registered by a party-centered
analysis of the election.

Primordial Ties and the Periphery

Electoral systems, like other social institutions, are culturally constituted. One finds differences in the meanings of institutions such as
elections not only between countries but also
within them.[12] Erguder and Hofferbert's examination of two decades of elections in Turkey highlights the importance of regionalism in accounting
for electoral outcomes. In so doing, they question the applicability of western party theory
which either implicitly or explicitly assumes that
political competition is characterized by a single
dominant dimension, usually a class or left-right
axis which structures competition according to economic issues. Party theory further assumes that
this is a pre-requisite for a pattern of orderly
moderation of conflict in a setting of consensus
(Downs 1957). However, as Erguder and Hofferbert
point out, political competition in modernizing
societies is rarely characterized by a single dominant dimension.[13] For example, in the societies
discussed in this volume political competition is

multidimensional--organized around traditional/
modern and/or center/periphery axes as well as
emergent class divisions. In Turkey, fragmentation and uncertainty about patterns of support has
been worse in the periphery, with most of the personalistic parties there (e.g. NAP and NSP). The
ultra-left or ultra-right have been also been
strongest in the central Anatolian plateau--the
most geographically inaccessible region, and the
one with the highest concentration of non-Turkish
groups. Erguder and Hofferbert see Ozal's appeal
to traditional values as crucial in enabling his
victorious Motherland Party to absorb and thus diminish the impetus toward fragmentation on the periphery.

As mentioned above, Israeli parties have attempted to exploit (or accomodate if you will),
the kin-based loyalties among Arabs in Israel for
some time. In the 1985 Israeli elections Labor
abandoned separate token factions and put Arabs on
its own List.[14] It is difficult to be certain
whether the weakening of the importance of clan
ties is a cause or consequence of this policy.

In Egypt, kin ties (*asabiyyah*) are credited
for the substantially higher level of voter participation in the rural areas and also blamed for
the higher incidence of electoral fraud there.
The government dismissed reports of fraud as "in-
evitable in a society where, especially in the
countryside 'tribal' or family loyalties and ri-
valries still loom large" (Hendriks 1985:12). Unfortunately, we do not have case material of how
kin-based loyalties were actually operationalized
in specific contexts.

Gavrielides (this volume) argues that tribal
organization is especially well-suited to democratic processes because of the tribal emphasis on
egalitarian values, traditional access to leaders,
and an indigenous (kin-based) representative
structure. Rather than being politically back-
ward, Gavrielides maintains that in Kuwait where
political parties are illegal, tribes served as an
indigenous and legal form of political organization which enabled them to conduct primary
elections, the first to be held in Kuwait's history.

Political action such as voting in a national election may "speak" in the idiom of local values. Elements of traditional leadership styles can be combined in new ways in new settings. The cases presented in this book and those referred to in this introduction should serve as examples of the many meanings such ties can have in the context of democratic elections. The Jordanian case (Chapter 5) indicates that it is too simple to say that clan ties are more important in some elections than others, or in one period more than another. The social bases of political support are often diverse and no single, inherent feature of one's being will automatically insure loyalty. As Rosen has put it for Morocco,

> although one should in theory be able to rely on the help of close kinsmen for any particular venture, in point of fact there is a wide range of permissible be- havior associated with any inherent re- lationship and that it is, therefore, both possible and necessary to contract and not merely implement a wide network of personal ties that have been formed with individual members of one's own kin group as well as with outsiders (Rosen 1972:219).

Role of Religion

Islamic fundamentalism was an important ele- ment in the elections in Egypt, Jordan, and Ku- wait. Moench focuses on the growing strength of Islamic Fundamentalists in Egypt as being one of the most serious threats to Egypt's stability.[15] He cites the weakness of the political Left out- side of intellectual circles is indirect evidence of the growing strength of the Islamic groups since the Left-wing parties and the Islamic asso- ciations must draw on the same constituency for popular support. Both of the important parties of the Left, Tagammu' and 'Amal, addressed Islamic themes in their campaign. The endorsement of Westernization by the NDP and the New Wafd will in

12

Moench's opinion produce a more militant reaction
among the members of Egypt's Islamic associations
and he concludes that in the long run, any state
defined in terms of religious criteria includes
contradictions that are destabilizing.

Because of the recent trend toward Islamic
fundamentalism throughout the Middle East, "Islamic" candidates in Jordan received a great deal of
attention in the Jordanian press. However, as I
point out in Chapter 5, the success of the two so-
called "Islamic" candidates is related, not so
much to religious matters, but to the candidate's
more militant position on Palestine and Israel
than that of many of their opponents.

In Kuwait both the Shia and Sunni Fundamentalists faired rather poorly in the 1985 election.
The alliance between the Shia and the Sunnis broke
down in 1976 and this combined with the effects of
redistricting severly limited their chances in this
last election.

In Israel there was continued fragmentation
of Orthodox religious parties which resulted in a
set back for the National Religious Party. Like
Jordan's Islamic candidates, Mier Kahane's Kach,
which broke the 1% minimum for the first time, received more media exposure than due 1.2% of the
votes. Although the total number of Orthodox
Knesset members remained about the same, the fragmentation of the orthodox block into five parties
diminished their strength.

Electoral Reforms

Because electoral systems are culturally constituted, they are continually produced and repro-
duced. (See Layne 1986a for an elaboration of
this process.) The emergent quality of electoral
systems, one of the most important themes of this
book, is perhaps most obvious in the process of
electoral reforms.

The Turkish 1982 Constitution, while retaining the broad contours of proportional representation (e.g., party list systems), imposed severe
limitations on the entry of minor parties in an
effort to reduce fragmentation. Substantial minimum percentages are required at both the local and

national level before seats may be obtained by any
participating party.

In Israel, the near stalemate between Likud
and Labor reawakened public discussion of electoral reform. Proposals included raising the minimum
number of votes required for representation in
parliament from 1 to 5 percent, (a measure that
would have eliminated all but three parties from
the eleventh Knesset), establishment of a system
combining electoral districts with the existing
system of proportional representation. National
lists would require a larger number of votes for
election which would be disadvantageous to smaller
parties, encouraging them to unite in larger voting blocs.

Egypt instituted a national minimum of 8% and
contemplated one as high as 10%. Any party which
did not succeed in winning 8% of the vote nationally forfeited its votes to the front-runner.
Combined party lists were banned. As the case of
Egypt clearly points out, in addition to the number of adherents each candidate has, the turnout
of the adherents of each and the distribution of
the adherents of each among the voting districts
may substantially determine the fortunes of candidates. (See also Hendriks 1985:16 on consequences
of party lists in Egypt.)

In Jordan the 1984 parliamentary by-elections
served as a case on which to base electoral reforms in preparation for full parliamentary
elections, now expected in 1988. A draft of the
new electoral law was submitted by the government
to Parliament in January 1986. A number of amendments were made by the Lower House and the revised
law was approved in March and passed on to the Upper House which endorsed it with no further amendments on April 28, 1986. The law raised the number of deputies from sixty to 142, lowered the
voting age from twenty to nineteen, and raised the
nomination fee for candidates from JD 65 to JD
500.

Gavrielides explores in detail the repercus-
sions of the changes instituted in Kuwait's electoral system in 1981. He maintains that the new
system of election districts was designed to and
indeed succeeded in enhancing the strength of the
Sabah's tribal supporters at the expense of the

14

Merchants and the Shia.[16] This attempt at balanc-
ing the power of different social groups may have
backfired. The "coalition of 27" tribal members
of parliament proved a powerful and outspoken
group which may have been one of the elements
leading to the suspension of parliament.

Recent Middle Eastern Elections

It is hoped that the analyses of these recent
Middle Eastern elections will enhance our understanding and appreciation of the ways that seem-
ingly similar institutions can have different
meanings in different social contexts. A vote is
a symbolic act and by definition therefore multi-
vocal and multi-valent. Several of the chapters
draw attention to the role kin ties play along
with party allegiances and center/periphery and
class cleavages in electoral politics. They serve
as a caution against the temptation to compartmen-
talize or typologize constituencies ("tribal" or
"modern") or to assume that social cleavages do
not crosscut one another. The challenge is to understand the meanings that the multiplicity of social attachments and various sources of collective
identity have in a particular context and how
these meanings inform one another. One of the
aims of this book has been to move beyond simple
characterizations of political systems to understand the complexities of social ties which shape
both electoral systems and electoral behavior.

Notes

[1] For an example of difference in parliamentary elites see Tachau's (1980) comparison of parliamentary representatives in Turkey, Lebanon, and
Israel.
[2] While all elections are collective representations, the style and tone of the public performance varies from culture to culture. For example, on the South Pacific Island of Ponape the
cultural value is one of masking one's intentions
in order not to offend another by disagreement or
worse, to attempt to directly influence another
adult's behavior (Petersen 1985:38-41). Thus, Po-
napeans were offended by the radio campaign

speeches the day before the election which tried
to sway their votes. In contrast, in Jordan and
Crete and Egypt (at least in the rural areas) people make public their intentions. Of course, because of secret balloting, there is nothing to assure that people will vote as they say they will.
Nevertheless, in these two face-to-face communities people's opinions are well known and often
flaunted. (See Hendriks 1985:13,14).

[3] For instance, the 1985 Israeli Knesset
elections embodied the contradictory Israeli conceptions of the state as Jewish-Zionist and as
democratic. Erguder and Hofferbert note the effects of the fragmentation of Turkish party politics on the traditional Ottoman conception of the
state which is seen as functioning to combat centrifugal tendencies in an empire characterized by
a complex social mosaic of ethnic and religious
groups. Eickelman (1985) also perceives changes
in the way state authority is practically elabo-
rated and experienced in Morocco. The state apparatus was traditionally considered unpredictable,
to be approached cautiously through intermediaries
capable of securing favorable decisions on one's
behalf. Whereas, since the 1977 parliamentary
elections, political accountability and public debate of at least local issues emerged as an alternative to the politics of notables (1986:194). He
sees the rising educational level of Morocco's
population to have a corresponding tendency to
hold the state to the letter of what it formally
declares to be the rights of its citizens
(1986:193).

[4] The term landslide entered the language of
politics in the nineteenth century and has come to
mean any particularly one-sided election. In the
United States the term has been technically applied to cases in which a Presidential candidate
lost no more than 20% of the states or carried 80%
of the electoral votes or at least 53% of the popular vote (Kelley 1983:26). According to this
definition, twenty-four of the forty-six presidential contests which took place up until 1972 were
landslides. For example, Kelley's analysis of
voters' attitudes in the 1964 and 1972 American
presidential elections shows that Nixon's "landslide" victory was very much less sure than that
of Johnson and owed less to positive evaluations

of Nixon by voters than it did to negative evaluations of his opponent (Kelley 1983:36, 42).

[5] See also Celine (1985).

[6] See Owen (1983) on Mubarak's dilemma concerning Egypt's place in the Arab Oil Economy.

[7] But winning support of one *hamula* automatically antagonized other *hamulas* in the village.
MAPAI tried to overcome this by creating three
Arab lists and trying to assign one to each *hamula*.

[8] A vivid index of the relative importance of
the municipal and Knesset elections was that votes
for a *hamula* in the municipal election were traded
for votes for a party in the general elections at
an exchange rate of three general election votes
for one local vote.

[9] Although, like Warner's (1959) analysis of
the parade in Yankee City, Herzfeld is concerned
with collective representations, his approach is
more actor and action-oriented than Warner's Durk-
heimian model.

[10] Political parties did not play a significant role in Jordan's 1985 parliamentary by-
elections. All parties, save the Muslim Brotherhood are banned. Yet, as in the 1956 elections
outlawed parties could have played an important
role nonetheless. I argue that the fact that political parties were not important in the 1984
elections does not mean that this model of political representation has ceased to exist. It simply
reflects the fact that the Arab nationalist parties which were so popular in Jordan in the 1950s
and 1960s have proved to have little to offer in
the way of a solution to the primary concern of
the Jordanian public, namely the Israeli threat
and the freeing of the occupied territories including the holy city of Jerusalem. Hence, for
the moment, no existing party seemed worthy of
support. Many Jordanians still believe in parties
as the preferred form of political organization
and lament the lack of party politics in Jordan
today. Political parties are also illegal in Kuwait.

[11] Despite the fact that ethnic issues per
se, were much less salient in 1984 than they were
in 1981, Labor and Likud are becoming increasingly
divided along on ethnic lines. The movement to
militant right is especially important among Ori-

ental Jews. Orent argues that the linkage between Oriental Jews and the New Zionist right is enduring. She rejects predictions of a break by Oriental Jews from Herut and the creation of a seperatist political identity as Orientals. The power vacuum in Herut, Likud's dominant faction, created by Begin's political retirement described by Peretz and Smooha continues to be played out. The recent conflict within the Herut party during the party's convention, (the first to be held without the leadership of Menachem Begin), and the victory of Ariel Sharon over Begin's son, the subsequent coup in the party by Ariel Sharon and David Levy who represent the Sephardic voters strengthened the voice of Oriental Jews (*New York Times* 3-14-1986, 3-17-1986, 3-12-1986).

[12] Anthropological community-based studies are especially well-suited to address the effects of local or kin-based loyalties on participation within the state, an issue which emerges in several of the chapters of this volume.

[13] Indeed, one wonders whether this is ever really the case.

[14] (See Eloul 1985 for a discussion of the history of Bedouin lists).

[15] Hendriks (1985:15) on the other hand, saw the role of Islam in the campaign more an idiom for right-mindedness than important in terms of content. His observations in meetings in both rural and urban areas was that people were more concerned with their daily problems and issues of corruption, inflation, housing, subsidies or the International Monetary Fund.

[16] See Crystal 1985 for a penetrating discussion of the changes in Kuwait's ruling coalition since the exploitation of oil.

Chapter II

RESTORATION OF DEMOCRACY IN TURKEY? POLITICAL REFORMS AND THE ELECTIONS OF 1983

Ustun Erguder and Richard I. Hofferbert

Introduction: Problems and Diagnosis in 1980

Following over three years of military government, an election was held in November 1983 for a Turkish national parliament. Under a new constitution, approved by plebiscite in 1983, the election produced a civilian government headed by Prime Minister Turgut Ozal, based on a parliamentary majority for his Motherland Party. The constitution and the rules under which the November election was conducted represented a deliberate attempt on the part of the military directorate, headed by General Kenan Evren, to remold the electoral and partisan structure of Turkish political life. The question addressed in this study is: To what extent do the results of the 1983 election suggest that the effort succeeded in remolding the Turkish party system and electoral practices in such a way as to enhance the chances for a legitimate, democratic order?

Between 1978 and 1980, inflation had tripled, climbing into the three-digit range. Political murders and assassinations had reached frightening proportions--between twenty and thirty per day. Man hours lost to strikes multiplied eight times in two years. The trade deficit reached record proportions. On September 12, 1980 the military ousted the civilian coalition headed by Suleyman Demirel. Although surveys to confirm the impression are lacking, there is little evidence to suggest widespread popular disapproval of the military takeover. It was followed by a virtual elimination of visible violence, some reduction in inflation, and at least the appearance of a methodical strategy for returning to civilian, constitutional rule. In fact the results of the Constitutional Referendum of 1982, signaling the return to civilian rule, are probably a good report on the apparent mood of the Turkish populace/electorate. The voters seem to have treated the Referendum as a question of regime definition, with greater than 90 percent turnout and over 90 percent approval among participants.

Throughout the three years of military rule, and reaching a crescendo in the election campaign of November, 1983, the military's major spokesmen put principal blame for economic and civil deterioration generally on the political party system and specifically on the leaders who had been in place since the (militarily inspired) constitution of 1961. The expressed objective of the junta was to reform the structure of Turkish democracy. In addition to the restoration of civil order, the major instrument of political reform was to be a rewriting of electoral and parties laws. This statutory activity was supplemented by tight control over participation in the first National Assembly election under the new constitution.

Implicit in the military government's strategy, and explicit in much of its rhetoric, were a specific theory of the causes of Turkey's problems and a set of solutions to attack those causes. In that theory, party organizations and leadership behavior loomed large. Briefly it states that intense party competition, especially in the late 1970s, led to parliamentary and governmental immobility. That immobility, in turn, had important policy consequences, threatening the "State" and its perceived distinctive, traditional role as the anchor of the Turkish society (Mardin 1966). Immobility also derailed the contemporary function of the State as a modernizing agent. Long Ottoman history has provided the military leaders with an instinctive assessment that, whenever the center (the State) is not able to exert its authority in order to perform its traditional functions, centrifugal tendencies have shaken an empire characterized by a complex social mosaic of ethnic and religious groups.

The "transcendental" conception of the State as binding and virtually defining Turkish society (Heper n.d.) was under many threats in the 1970s. These challenges included (1) the lack of parliamentary majorities; (2) ever-changing coalition governments vulnerable to the threats and demands of ideological extremes; (3) excessive use of patronage by clientelistic parties, some of which were experiencing a share of governmental power for the first time; (4) the inability to lead or legislate effectively to deal with increasing economic woes and violence.[1]

The immediate culprits, in the eyes of the military, were, on the one hand, a set of institutions that seemed to have failed to fulfill their promise, and, on the other hand, a set of politicians who had failed to provide leadership. The pluralist aspects of the 1961 constitution, the parties, and the electoral system were the institutional villains. The politicians to blame included virtually everyone who had occupied a highly visible governmental or party role in the 1970s.

The thesis of this study is that, even though the manifest goal of the military government between 1980 and 1983 may have been to restrain the pluralist thrust of recent Turkish politics, the unintended consequence may have been to align the party system along a more modern dimension. The reforms may have set a framework conducive to the consensual conflict management supposedly characteristic of western democracies.

Prior to 1961, the procedure for electing members of the National Assembly was heavily biased toward the formation of large parliamentary majorities. The party whose list obtained a majority in each of the provinces received all of the seats from that province. For example, in Turkey's first free, competitive election in 1950, Adnan Menderes' Democrat Party (DP) received 53 percent of the vote but 86 percent of the seats. The Republican People's Party (RPP), which had been the sole legal party from 1923 through 1945, obtained only 13 percent of the seats for 39 percent of the votes. In 1954 and 1957, respectively, the DP received 93 and 70 percent of the seats for only 56 and 47 percent of the votes. A consequence of this was, at least in the eyes of the opposition, an excessive concentration and arbitrariness of executive power further aided by a constitution quite similar to the Westminster model, with its emphasis on parliamentary sovereignty, but lacking its unwritten constraints. The watershed was reached when the military intervened in 1960, deposed and executed Prime Minister Menderes, and, in 1961, imposed a new constitution.

Especially since the numerical and political imbalance of the 1950s operated to the disadvantage of the RPP (the party presumably carrying the tradition of Ataturk's revolution), the militarily inspired Constitution of 1961 imposed drastic reforms. It enshrined in basic law a long list of specific redistributive policy objectives--welfare, health care, etc. Among several key reforms aimed at checking the concentration of power was the adoption of proportional represention. Over the 1960s and 1970s, various experiments within the confines of proportional representation, had the effect of easing the entry of minor parties, some of which reflected meaningful cleavages in the society. The results that can be at least in part attributed to these post-1961 reforms will be discussed in some detail in the following section. Let it suffice to say here that, in the 1980s, the military government singled out these provisions as a prime target for reform.

The 1982 Constitution seems to be a reaction to its 1961 predecessor. The new document, with some overtones of presidentialism, emphasizes governmental authority as against legislative unruliness--a trait of the 1960s. While retaining the broad contours of proportional representation (e.g., party list systems), the 1982 Constitution imposed severe limitations on the entry of minor parties. Substantial minimum percentages are required at both the local and national level before seats may be obtained by any participating party.

In addition, for the parliamentary election of November, 1983, the military directorate screened all potential parties, banning all but three from actual competition. The directorate also proscribed participation and even public discussion of politics by hundreds of specified persons who had been prominent in pre-1980 Turkish government and politics.

Aside from the immediate impact on specific persons involved or excluded from the election of 1983, are there likely to be any detectable long-term systemic effects of these practices and reforms on Turkish political life? An examination of the conditions prior to 1983 is a prerequisite for answering this question.

Maladies of the Party System

Volatility. Our central objective is to test the impact of the party reforms implemented in the election of 1983. To do that, we must have a measure of the prior form. One answer is that there simply was not much form. The dominant feature of the Turkish political landscape between 1950 and 1980, but especially in rising magnitude through the 1960s and 1970s, was volatility in the bases of party support.

Pedersen (1979) has developed an index of "political volatility" for European elections between 1948 and 1977 based on individual parties' performance in successive elections.[2] The scoring procedure essentially indicates the ability to predict party fortunes in one election from their performance in the preceeding contest. The higher the score, the lower the predictability. The Western European scores average 8.1, with a range of 16.8 for France to 3.7 for Austria during the period from 1948-1977. Between 1950 and 1979, by comparison, Turkey's national volatility score averaged 19.3. Clearly, there is less "structure" in such a state of volatility.

National figures, of course, understate switching across parties, since there is much cancelling out. The lower the aggregation, the more revealing the data on such switching. Unfortunately, the time-series survey data that would give the most accurate rendition of the individual sources of volatility are not available.

Volatility at the national level was magnified among the sixty-seven Turkish provinces, with some provinces consistently scoring in the realm of 40.0. Others, however, were much more consistent in their partisanship, rarely exceeding 10.0.

Turkey's is, of course, a very recent experiment in democracy in a country that is, by any commonly accepted index, considerably less economically developed than any of the European examples included in Pedersen's analysis. If we had comparable data for other LDCs, even for those at a level relatively similar to Turkey, it is probable that Turkey's performance in the past generation and a half would not appear so relatively unstructured.

We are arguing that, accelerating in the late 1960s and through the 1970s, Turkey was going through a fundamental redefinition of the cleavages of political competition. While having not yet solved the National Revolution, as it would be termed by Lipset and Rokkan (1966), Turkey was fully in the throes of the Industrial Revolution. In fact, in the 1950s, Turkish politics briefly came rather close to having one dominant dimension expressed in the two-party competition between the Democrats (DP) and the Republican People's Party (RPP). That dimension was principally defined by the conflict between center and periphery (with undeniable overtones of more modern economic conflicts).

Competition in the 1950s came close to the Downsian model (1957), so far as it is possible to detect with aggregate data. A system operating nearly along the lines of that model would have relatively low political volatility. Marginal voters would be drawn in from the extremes of each of the competing entities. But a solid core of adherents would stick with the major competitors overtime, with many of them doing so as a choice of lesser evils. Unfortunately, the condition of Turkish politics into the 1960s and 1970s discouraged such a tidy pattern of accommodation.

Fragmentation and Polarization. Volatility is but one manifestation of the "Bermuda Triangle" through which Turkish democracy struggled in the 1970s. Linked to volatility were fragmentation and polarization, especially within governing elites.

Two major changes have been identified to explain increasing instability. First, the Turkish parliamentary system changed from, in Sartori's (1978) terms, a "predominant party system" to a hybrid between his "moderate" and "polarized pluralism."[3] Secondly, the patterns of party support[4] changed to such an extent that Ozbudun (1979) and Erguder (1981, 1982) have both labeled the 1970s as "critical" in Key's terms (Key 1955).

The "predominant party system" classification seems to fit the Turkish case during the 1950s and the 1960s. The Democrats and their successor, the Justice Party (JP), were able to stay in power by themselves during this era even though their electoral success was not of the same magnitude as that of, for example, the PRI in Mexico--a classic and extreme case of a "predominant party system." The only exception is the 1960-1965 period when the DP was deposed by the military coup of May, 1960. Even though there is some evidence that class based politics was becoming relevant in the seventies with the JP being identified with propertied interests (Ozbudun 1979), this "predominance" at the polls was based on the enduring center/periphery cleavage which helped broaden the spectrum of that party's appeal to include less privileged groups with traditional values, notably the peasantry and the urban marginals.

The 1961 election which followed the coup, did not produce a governmental majority, as three parties (the Justice Party, the New Turkey Party and the Republican Peasants Nation Party) were competing for the support of the adherents of the outlawed DP. The issue of succession was settled in 1965 when the JP received 53 percent of the total votes cast. The party system reverted to its predominant character. Both the electoral and parliamentary majorities, however, were not as comfortable as those of the 1950s.

The 1973 election signaled the end of the "predominant" party system in Turkey. The JP suffered its worst performance, with 30 percent of the votes. The RPP did much better, with 33.3 percent. It shifted towards an ideology of social democracy under the leadership of Bulent Ecevit in an attempt to change its long standing image as champion of both the state elites at the center and the traditional landed interests in the countryside. But the RPP did not capture enough seats to form a government alone. The 1973 election ushered in a new period of coalitions and governmental crises.

The curious aspect of the party system that emerged after the 1973 election is that it had all the formal trappings of Sartori's "moderate pluralism" in which alternating coalition governments around major parties are the rule of the day (Sartori 1978:173-185). In "moderate pluralism" the system is center-oriented in the sense that support for ideological poles is weak, both in terms of electoral support and parliamentary representation. "Moderate pluralism" somewhat resembles the British two-party system, with its moderation and lack of polarized or extremist politics. The major difference is in respect to alternation of governmental power. "Moderate pluralism" is characterized, as in contemporary West Germany, by alternative coalitions of governmental power revolving around two major parties, rather than alternation of power between two major parties, each governing alone when in power.

There was little electoral or parliamentary strength at the ideological poles in Turkey during the 1970s. The Turkish Unity Party, the only party to the left of the RPP that participated in the 1973 elections, got only 1.1 percent of the total votes, and it captured only one seat in the National Assembly. In 1977, the combined percentage of the parties to the left of the RPP did not exceed 0.5 percent of the votes, with no representation in the Assembly.

The situation to the right of the JP was more severely fragmented. The National Salvation Party (NSP) and the National Action Party (NAP) introduced an uncommon level of ideological disputation to Turkish politics. The NSP, focusing on fundamentalist Islamic issues and appealing to the Sunni elements in various parts of the country, polled 11.8 percent in 1973 and placed forty-eight deputies out of a total membership of 450 in the National Assembly. The NAP, appealing to an extreme right ideology with its emphasis on discipline, leadership, and militant party organization, stressed nationalism (with overtones of racism) and anti-communism. It polled 3.4 percent in 1973 and placed three deputies in the National Assembly. In 1977 these same parties polled 8.6 and 6.4 percent, winning twenty-four and sixteen seats respectively.

The other parties represented in the 1973 Assembly were the Democratic Party (DemP) with 11.9 percent (forty-five deputies) and the Republican Reliance Party (RRP) with 5.3 percent (thirteen deputies). These personalistic parties were not identified with ideological polarization. In 1977 each of these parties polled 1.9 percent, while gaining one (DemP) and three (RRP) deputies respectively.

The Turkish party system of the 1970s, however, performed much like Sartori's "polarized pluralist" systems despite the fact that, as detailed elsewhere, the ideological distance was not great between the two major parties, the JP and the RPP. Governmental instability and parliamentary immobility increased even more after the 1977 election, when the system, paradoxically, approximated more closely the formal aspects of "moderate pluralism," with the representation of ideological parties to the right of the JP being trimmed and the other minor parties of the right virtually disappearing.

Throughout the 1970s, ideological intransigence increased in the parliament, with growing inability of the major parties to come to terms on the basic rules of the game--despite the visible threats to the continuation of a competitive system. Concessions were bargained away allowing minor party coalition participation far disproportionate to their electoral strength, especially by the NSP and the NAP (Heper n.d.; Sunar and Sayari n.d.).

Party discipline seemed to break down as defections from one party to another and the making and unmaking of coalition governments became increasingly rewarding. Consequently, governmental leadership based on secure parliamentary majorities, critically important for dealing with mounting economic problems as well as with rising social and political unrest, virtually disappeared. The behavior of the Turkish party system was reminiscent of Germany during the Weimar Republic, a classic case of "polarized pluralism." The conditions appeared increasingly threatening to the ideological fabric of the Turkish Republic, extolling a powerful state, making especially the military elite quite apprehensive.

What made the Turkish parliamentary party
system behave in such a curious manner, leading to
the instability of the political system? Sunar
and Sayari focus on ideological polarization and
fragmentation as the chief culprits (Sunar and Sayari n.d.). Polarization of political parties and
their leaders is not a new phenomenon in Turkey.
In fact, the breakdown of the democratic system in
1960, prior to the May military intervention,
could be partially explained by the intransigence
of the DP leadership toward the opposition and to
the extreme oppositional stance assumed by the
RPP. These postures virtually eliminated that
consensual politics which is so critically important for a viable parliamentary democracy.[5] Novel
in the 1970s was the increasingly ideological tint
this polarization assumed, especially between the
RPP and the JP.

In contrast to polarization, fragmentation of
the party system is of more recent origin, increasing gradually during the 1960s, when compared
with the earlier period, and building through the
1970s. In the 1960s, the evidence was an increased number of parties in the Assembly (four in
1961, six in 1965, and eight in 1969), along with
increasing difficulty in keeping party discipline.
This fragmentation, however, did not have a major
impact on the party system, since the JP was able
to maintain its predominance in the elections of
1965 and 1969, returning parliamentary majorities
each time.

The destabilizing impact of fragmentation in
the party system came into full force in the 1973
election when no party could return a governing
majority to the National Assembly. The 1977
elections provided no cure. In the atmosphere of
heightened volatility, polarization, and fragmentation in the 1960s and the 1970s were tearing the
Turkish party system asunder.

While always noting the effects of formal
electoral rules and individual leaders' behavior,
the search for causes of fragmentation in the
Turkish party system almost always overlooks one
other important factor--the impact of military interventions every decade. Each military intervention, while ostensibly responding to political
misbehavior, creates itself a period of uncertain-

ty and fragmentation in the party system. The banning of the DP in 1960 ushered in a four-year period of coalition governments in the Assembly and a disorganized scramble for votes among the electorate, especially among groups seeking to inherit the mantle of the Democrat Party. Even though no specific punitive action was taken against any of the political parties after the 1971 military intervention, the election that followed in 1973 brought in the DemP, the NAP, and the NSP as electoral contenders.

The military intervention of 1980 and the electoral/party arrangements that followed were designed to end the fragmentation of the party system which the military leaders identified as a culprit in Turkish political problems. Paradoxically, the banning of the old parties and leaders, and the emergence of new ones, coupled with an electoral system designed to limit the number of parties in the Assembly, might usher in yet another period in which fragmentation of the parliamentary party system will be reduced while fragmentation of the electoral party system will be increased, at least until patterns of partisanship stabilize. This is a limitation on our ability to project systemic consequences from the first election under the new rules.

One may, of course, imagine various scenarios of political instability which may emerge under such a dual party system, where the extraparliamentary parties are not coincident with those in parliament. Military interventions appear to be associated with the fragmentation, or, if one prefers, with the creation of uncertainty that destabilizes the Turkish party system. In other words, every military intervention sows the seeds of the next intervention by destabilizing the parties and thus the political system.

One point needs to be stressed here: Any fragmentation or uncertainty after military interventions appears to occur at the right of the political spectrum. In 1961, if one may consider the RPP in those years as relatively left, given its emphasis on "etatism," the fragmentation both at the electoral and parliamentary levels took place to the right of the RPP. After 1971, the fragmentation was exclusively at the right. Similarly, in the post-1980 period, the major uncertainty with respect to the patterns of support appeared to be at the right of the spectrum. This might turn out to be one of the most important political problems facing Turkey during the 1980s. That is, a "modern" political system does not function smoothly merely because a unified, class-based left is in place. It is also critically dependent upon a coherent, moderate, pro-system conservative party with a sufficient promise of capacity to win, in order to keep quiescent the otherwise extremist forces of the Right.

Volatility, fragmentation, and polarization of the party system help explain the gross instability of the Turkish political system during the 1970s. They also explain the frame of mind of the military in pushing a constitutional overhaul to limit office-seeking and to reshape the party system so that the 1980s would not be molded to the pattern of the 1970s.

On the other hand, a close look into changing patterns of party support not only provides an explanation for the woes of the 1970s, but it also sheds light on possible outcomes with respect to party support during the 1980s--with totally new parties and leaders competing. It is our contention that what made the Motherland Party electoral coalition possible in 1983 was the fact that the Turkish electorate of the previous decade was already groping for a new centrist solution to the maladies of the party system.

To increase the accuracy of our analysis of the 1983 election, it is necessary to construct some quantitative benchmarks of partisan structure in the preceeding two decades. Along the way, these measures will serve to enumerate and validate the verbal description of the party system which we have provided above.

Measuring Post-1961 Partisan Structure

By analyzing the patterns of party performance in the Turkish provinces, we may get a more accurate picture of the dimensionality running through this electoral history. It would be most useful to have a series of surveys to identify the bases of individual partisanship and persistance of electoral behavior. Unfortunately, such data are not available in anything approaching consistent form. Reliable and quite relevant aggregate data are available, however, for the sixty-seven provinces.

Our use of provincial data is not wholly a compromise. If there is any persisting pattern to recent Turkish politics, it is reasonable to assume that the pattern is related to an organizational and socioeconomic context measurable with provincial-level aggregate data.

Turkish provinces (*Iller*) are not comparable to states in a federal system. They are administrative units, more similar to French departments than to American states or Swiss cantons. Nevertheless, each jurisdiction does represent some degree of socioeconomic coherence. They serve as units for the delivery of public services. And they constitute, for most parties, a unit of organization. Given the rather high quality of social, economic, and political statistics in Turkey, at a minimum provincial data capture a good portion of any major geographic variance. And, with Turkey's geography, that variance is of no mean consequence.

To take advantage of cross-provincial variance as an aid to gaining insight into the patterning or structuring of pre-1980 Turkish politics, we conducted a pooled factor analysis of party voting percentages across the provinces for four national parliamentary elections: 1965, 1969, 1973, and 1977. Several minor parties were grouped together, given that individually their performance was quite skewed, even if highly variant across provinces, while their absolute percentages were very small. Two groups of minor parties were incorporated into the analysis: (1) minor left parties and (2) minor personalistic parties. In addition, we included the individual provincial percentages for the Justice Party, the National Action Party, the National Salvation Party, and the Republican People's Party. The percentages achieved in each set are indicated in Table 2.1.

The results of the factor analysis are presented in Table 2.2.

The first factor is a close approximation of Lipset and Rokkan's conception of a periphery/center
cleavage (1966:9-13). The modernizing, more or
less free market Justice Party anchors the scale
at the center end, followed closely by the equally
modernization-oriented Republican People's Party.
Only in 1965 did the RPP slip below any party other than the Justice Party on the periphery/center
factor. At the peripheral end of the scale are
the minor personalistic parties, along with the
heavily Islamic-oriented National Salvation Party.

The strength of the peripheral parties is
concentrated away from the sea coasts, along the
Syrian-Iraqi-Iranian border. This is not only the
most geographically inaccessible and topographi-
cally harsh part of Turkey, but also the region
where there is the highest concentration of ethno-
linguistic minority groups (Kurds, etc.) The only
apparent deviations are the central Anatolian
provinces of Konya and Kirsehir, which have been
bastions of religious dissent for centuries, most
notably focused around the Mevlevi (the order of
the Dervishes).

Unlike their proximity on the modern or center end of the first factor, the RPP and the JP
became polar opposites on the left/right dimen-
sion--the factor most comparable to the dominant
western party cleavage. The left/right dimension
is the most difficult to capture with aggregate
data because, by its very definition, it is less
territorial and more class relevant than is the
center-periphery dimension (Lipset and Rokkan
1967). The industrial commercial centers support
the left (e.g., Istanbul, Izmir, Adana, Ankara).
Support for the left comes from provinces which
had, in the 1970s, experienced Alevi/Sunni conflicts.

Repeated iterations of the data consistently
supported our observations indicating the necessity for accommodating a third factor into the analysis. Turkish electoral politics has been more
than a two dimensional rotation around a durable
periphery/center and an emerging left/right cleavage. These conflicts take place more or less
within the generally accepted structure of the regime, even if producing vigorous dissent from certain rules and tendencies of that regime. Even

the spokespersons of the minor personalistic parties, so strongly anchored at the peripheral end
of Factor 2, insisted upon their allegiance to the
Turkish state. But there are, within recent history and in the contemporary setting, persons and
groups who have not been so clear and firm in
their acceptance of the national regime.

Elements of Pan-Turanism--seeking unity of
the ethno-linguistic Turks of the world (including
more people outside the boundary of the Turkish
Republic than within)--persist just below the surface of many disputes in today's Turkey. The
Young Turk movement of the early years of the century was led by the Pan-Turanist Enver Pasha.

Notably, Factor 3, which we have labeled
"Anti-System," is one-tailed in its composition.
The National Action Party dominates this dimension, followed by the National Salvation Party in
one election, and a set of minor left parties. It
is the proximity of these minor left parties to
the "ultra-rightist" NAP that convinces us of the
value of the index as a measure of "anti-system"
political leanings. The negative (or "Pro-System") variance is modest, being anchored by the
Justice Party in 1973. But most of the pro-system
variance in the total matrix of elections and parties was concentrated in the first two factors:
periphery/center and left/right.

The factor analysis produces scores that are
uncorrelated with each other ("orthogonally rotat-
ed"). Thus, the score of a province on one factor
is computed holding constant the other two factors. A high score on periphery/center, therefore, does not mean that there are no anti-system
or left/right elements located there. Rather, it
reflects the *relative* amount of anti-system behavior, controlling for the extent of the other two
dimensions. The degree of anti-system voting,
relative to either periphery/center or left/right
behavior, was highest in the central Anatolian
plateau, but reaching from Afyon in the west of
Anatolia to Erzurum in the east.

Across the four elections--1965, 1969, 1973,
and 1977--included in the factor analysis, it is
interesting that there is no apparent time trend
in the loadings. Parties which earlier scored
high on one end or the other of the center-periph-

ery dimension do not move, in later elections, to a different factor. To the extent that aggregate data can reveal such a change, these findings suggest that there was no major realignment of electoral behavior in the decade and one half prior to the 1980 military take-over. Rather, there was a complex process of deterioration in system capacity.

The 1983 Election--Reinstatement or Reform?

An interesting aspect of the 1983 election is that it came in the wake of a Constitutional Referendum which may have had all the trappings of a regime endorsement. The question in November 1983 was: Will the electorate continue to give support to the military leaders by endorsing political parties favored by them or would politics and political cleavages become once again salient? The voters in 1983 have reverted from regime issues to *politics*, but the efforts of the military rulers to reshape and restructure politics appears at least tentatively to have had an impact.

Previous efforts by Turkish military governments to alter the structure of the party system have a mixed record. The banning of the Democrats in 1960 did not prevent a reincarnation in the form of the Justice Party. On the other hand, the reforms in electoral systems embodied in the 1961 Constitution almost certainly accelerated the fragmentation and polarization of Turkish politics--a hardly intended, even if predictable, outcome of the constitution writers' efforts.

Did the conditions imposed on the election of 1983 actually bring about a realignment along a newly dominant cleavage? One event does not make a trend, of course, and it will not be possible to confirm a pattern until much more time has passed. The election of 1961 proved to be a poor predictor of future patterns, since the supporters of the ousted DP were casting about among several groups seeking to inherit the DP mantle. The 1983 election could appear to be an equally poor predictor.[6] We think not, however, given the controls imposed upon the available options. All previous parties were banned, and their supporters' choices were limited to three options--the Motherland Party (headed by Turgut Ozal, the current prime minister), the Populist Party (thought by some to be a potential successor to the RPP), and the National Democratic Party (given tacit support by the leaders of the military government).

The returns from 1983 certainly do not conform to the old pattern, not even as it could have been predicted to evolve from the trends in place in the late 1970s. By many standards, the results in 1983 deviate from the past even more than in the volatile, fragmented conditions evolving under the pre-1980 system. A review of the conditions and participation rules of that election is in order here. Recall that the military government had taken several steps to break the old pattern:

1. Disbanding and prohibiting the re-formation of all parties from the previous period

2. Screening all potential parties and proscribing all but three from participation in 1983--The Motherland Party, the Populist Party, and the National Democratic Party

3. Proscribing from standing for parliamentary seats a specific list of named politicians from previous governments

4. Imposing, through the Constitution, an electoral system heavily loaded against minor parties

The results gave Ozal's Motherland Party (MP) 45 percent of the popular vote and 211 seats out of a total of 400 in the new National Assembly. This is Turkey's first majority government since 1969. President Evren congratulated the winners, accepted the results with grace, allowing the Prime Minister to be the de facto leader of the governing Cabinet.

The Populist party placed second, with 30 percent of the vote and 117 seats. The blessing of the military government was insufficient to enable the National Democrats to play a major role, with 24 percent and seventy-one seats.

As interesting as the absolute results, is
the extent to which any or all of the parties participating in 1983 seemed to "replace" parties
from the pre-1980 period. There is little question that the Justice Party, by 1965, was appealing to the same voters of the same socioeconomic
groups as did the Democrats of the pre-1961 period, despite the banning of the Democrats in 1961.
The Republican People's Party had carried the banner of Ataturk consistently from the one-party
period before 1950 all the way into the banning of
parties in 1980. Some speculated that the National Democrats would draw from the more right-wing
elements of the Justice Party, as well as the parties of the periphery, if not the anti-system parties.

Table 2.3 presents the correlations between
the 1983 votes and the factor scores of the three
dimensions of partisanship. The most important
message of Table 2.3 is that the MP--the clear
winner of the 1983 election--is not the anchor of
any pre-existing partisan cleavage. It comes
closest to the center end of the periphery/center
cleavage, but not with anything like the strength
of association of the now-outlawed Justice Party.

The volatility of Turkish parties' perform-
ance--the lack of consistent support among voting
groups--makes assessment of continuity or change
quite risky. It is difficult to sort the signal
from the noise of pre-1980 electoral behavior.
Without assuming what we wish to investigate,
namely the continuity or change in the bases of
support of the new parties compared to the old
ones, it is risky to draw conclusions from the
correlations of the 1983 election with specific
party figures in prior years. To the extent that
there was any stability in the pre-1980 period, we
are persuaded that it is captured better by the
three factors (periphery/center, left/right, anti-
system) than by votes in specific elections.
Therefore, while noting the correlations of the
1983 results with particular parties in prior
elections, we have the most confidence in the relations of 1983 to the provincial scores on the
three factors.

Turgut Ozal's Motherland Party, while captur-
ing nearly a majority of the votes (47 percent)

and an absolute majority of the seats in the new-
ly-constituted National Assembly, is not the reincarnation of any single pre-existing partisan entity. It is moderately anchored on the center end
of the periphery/center dimension (r = -.32), as
well as to the right of the left/right factor (r =
-.36). Most important, however, is the .50 correlation with the anti-system dimension of the 1960s
and 1970s.

The initial temptation is to read a gloomy
message in the correlation between the 1983 returns for the MP and the anti-system parties of
the pre-1980 period. We are more inclined, however, to see the glass as half full. The fragmentation of the party system of the 1960s and 1970s,
coupled with the absence of an acceptable center,
in effect pushed some elements of the electorate
to the edges of the system. Ozal's party, if it
can be viewed as a centrist, moderate force, has
served to drawback into the mainstream those who
were formerly engaged in anti-system protest. The
.44 and .36 correlation between the MP and the National Action Party in 1977 and 1973 respectively,
provides further confirmation of this observation.
The open question is: Were the anti-system voters
of the 1960s and 1970s forced into that stance before 1980 by the conditions of that time, or were
they forced by the military government's banning
of options in 1983 into support of the MP?

Optimists will accept the former interpretation. Whether the formerly discontented elements
stay within the fold of a centrist party will, in
all likelihood, hinge upon perceptions of the performance of Ozal's party in office.[7]

Less difficult to interpret is the performance of the Populist Party. It's support seems
solidly anchored on the left of the left/right dimension (r = .68). Recalling that the party most
strongly associated with that dimension was the
RPP, it is not surprising also that the Populists'
vote in 1983 correlates positively with the RPP
percentages in the two last elections before 1980
(r = .68 and .69, respectively).

While drawing moderately from the periphery
(r = .38) as well as from the right (r = .31), the
National Democratic Party--favorite of the military in the 1983 election--did not capture the

anti-system vote (-.39). It did, however, capitalize on some carry-over from the fragmentation of the pre-1980 period, being most closely associated with the minor personalistic splinter parties of 1973 (r = .45) and 1977 (r = .47).

When faced with a moderate option, disassociated from the tarnished politics of the past, the Turkish electorate seems to have responded positively. In the campaign of 1983, Turgut Ozal ran on a platform stressing economic growth and fiscal caution. He advocated de-emphasis on state economic enterprises. He has described himself as a devotee of "supply-side economics." His program would have placed him comfortably within the range of many western right-of-center parties. He also stressed the need to enhance Turkey's place within the Middle Eastern economic network. Sometimes described as a "Moslem technocrat," he seems to appeal to traditional values without giving them ideological preeminence over the need to bring Turkey into the international competitive marketplace. A comparison to Ronald Reagan is not wholly out of place. Reagan's appeal to Christian values, anti-abortion interests, etc. enables him to absorb traditional elements of the electorate without sacrificing his prime emphasis on modern issues--the market over the state, investment and growth over income maintenance programs, etc. Those who support Reagan for his economic policies may wince, but they tolerate his moral preachings in the quest of a winning coalition. Ozal's public stance on traditional morality--there in an Islamic garb--has, if anything, been notably more muted than that of his American counterpart. Ozal would seem, therefore, to be moving toward an absorption, and thus a diminution, of the impetus toward fragmentation on the periphery.

During the 1970s, while there was some fragmentation on the left, the RPP had moved steadily toward a solid, class-based foundation in the electorate. It was increasingly similar, in rhetoric and electoral appeal, if not in policy accomplishments, to a left-of-center social democratic party, with minimal relevance to more traditional lines of cleavage. What fragmentation there was on the left was probably due to immoderation of specific leaders, plus facilitation by the elec-

toral system. The new Populist Party of 1983 continued to capitalize on the growing coherence of
the left-of-center elements of the electorate.

Although the left splinter groups were often
dramatic in their ideological pronouncements and
protest behavior, their numbers and institutional
strength were less than the fragmentation on the
right. That is, the match between the RPP, as a
substantively moderate left party, and an enduring
set of electoral interests was greater than for
any single entity to the right-of-center. It was
on the right that the most threatening fragmentation had become most institutionalized.

Modernization in a competitive democratic
framework cannot be accomplished by a social democratic force alone. The right and the periphery
must have legitimate options *within the system*.
Ozal's Motherland Party may have provided a broad-
ly acceptable, pro-system alternative, neutraliz-
ing (for the time being, at least) and reintegrat-
ing if not eliminating the anti-systemic
tendencies in Turkish political life. If he and
his colleagues sustain the perception of putting
Turkey back on the slope of economic growth, with
reasonable domestic tranquility, and if they are
not derailed by international economic shocks,
Turgut Ozal may be facing an historic opportunity
to umpire Turkey's entry into the community of
democratic, materially prospering nations.

TABLE 2.1

Party Performance in Turkish National Assembly Elections, 1965-1977

Party	1965 %Vote	Seats	1969 %Vote	Seats	1973 %Vote	Seats	1977 %Vote	Seats
JP	52.9	240	46.5	256	29.7	149	36.9	189
RPP	28.8	134	27.4	143	33.3	185	41.4	213
NSP	---	---	---	---	11.8	48	8.6	24
NAP	---	---	3.2	1	3.4	3	6.4	16
Min-Pers*	15.4	62	17.6	40	21.8	65	6.2	8
Min-Left**	3.0	14	5.5	10	---	---	.5	---

* Republican Reliance Party, Republican Peasants' Nationalist Party, Democratic Party, Nationalist Party, New Turkey Party, Independenedents.

** For 1965, Turkish Labor Party. For other elections sum of Turkish Union Party and Turkish Labor Party.

Legend: Min-Pers = Minor Personalistic Parties
NSP = National Salvation Party
Trk Lab = Turkish Labor Party
RPP = Republican People's Party
Min-Left = Minor Left Parties
NAP = National Action Party
JP = Justice Party

41

TABLE 2.2

Structure of Turkish Party System:
Factor Analysis of Party Performance, 1965-1977

Factor Loadings/Party-Election					
Periphery/Center		Left/Right		Anti-System	
Min-Pers'69	.92	RPP'73	.86	NAP'77	.91
Min-Pers'77	.79	RPP'77	.85	NAP'73	.75
Min-Pers'65	.77	Min-Left'69	.66	NSP'73	.68
NSP'77	.76	Trk Lab'65	.60	Min-Left'69	.37
Min-Pers'73	.73	RPP'65	.57	Min-Left'77	.31
NSP'73	.30	Min-Left'77	.56	Min-Pers'65	.13
Trk Lab'65	.17	RPP'69	.47	NSP'77	.09
RPP'65	.12	NAP'77	.06	Min-Pers'69	.01
Min-Left'69	.03	NAP'73	-.03	JP'65	-.04
NAP'77	.00	Min-Pers'69	-.14	JP'69	-.07
Min-Left'77	-.02	JP'65	-.17	Trk Lab'65	-.07
NAP'73	-.09	Min-Pers'65	-.20	RPP'77	-.09
RPP'73	-.28	NSP'73	-.20	RPP'73	-.13
RPP'69	-.38	Min-Pers'77	-.23	JP'77	-.15
RPP'77	-.39	NSP'77	-.24	Min-Pers'73	-.18
JP'73	-.70	Min-Pers'73	-.33	RPP'65	-.20
JP'77	-.80	JP'69	-.37	RPP'69	-.21
JP'69	-.85	JP'73	-.45	Min-Pers'77	-.25
JP'65	-.88	JP'77	-.48	JP'73	-.32

Legend: Min-Pers = Minor Personalistic Parties (Listed in Table 2.1)
NSP = National Salvation Party
Trk Lab = Turkish Labor Party
RPP = Republican People's Party
Min-Left = Minor Left Parties (Listed in Table 2.1)
NAP = National Action Party
JP = Justice Party

TABLE 2.3

Relationship (r) Between 1983 Election and Prior Patterns:
Sixty-Seven Turkish Provinces

	Motherland	Populist	National Democratic
Periphery/Center	-.32	.02	.38
Left/Right	-.36	.68	-.31
Anti-System	.50	-.20	-.39
1973 & 1977 Elections			
JP '77	.36	-.24	-.15
JP '73	.18	-.18	.01
RPP '77	-.29	.68	-.39
RPP '73	-.38	.69	-.30
NAP '77	.44	-.17	-.35
NAP '73	.36	-.11	-.30
NSP '77	-.06	-.34	.42
NSP '73	.47	-.38	-.18
Min-Pers '77	-.27	-.13	.47
Min-Pers '73	-.20	-.21	.45
Min-Left '77	-.07	.32	-.24
Min-Left '73*			

* The minor left parties obtained an inconsequential number
of votes in 1973, nearly all endorsing the RPP.

Notes

[1] See Mardin (1969 and 1973) on the relationship of state and society. For a discussion of the problems of Turkish democracy during the 1970s see Karpat (1981).

[2] Referring to Escher and Tarrow (1975:480-481), Pedersen defines electoral volatility as "...the net change within the electoral party system resulting from individual vote transfers" (1979:3). Pedersen measures electoral volatility by aggregating the changes in the percentages of votes obtained by each party from one election to the next. If we let:

$P_{i, t}$ = percent vote obtained by party "i" at election "t"

then the change ("$\wedge$") in the strength of party "i" will be measured by:

$$\wedge P_{i,t} = P_{i,t} - P_{i,t-1}.$$

The total net change (TNC_t) in the party system is measured by (sign differences not considered):

$$TNC_t = Sum_{i=t} [\wedge P_{i,t}]$$

Cautioning the reader "...that the net gains from winning parties numerically are equal to the net losses of the parties that were defeated in the election...", Pedersen, finally, uses the following formula "...as slightly easier to calculate and to interpret..." to measure volatility (V):

$$V_{(t)} = \tfrac{1}{2} \times TNC_t, \text{ where } 0 \le V_t \le 100.$$

[3] For similar conclusions on this point see Sayari (1978:129-209) and Erguder (1982:97-138). For a slightly different interpretation of Sartori's typologies see Ozbudun (1985:262-281). On fragmentation and polarization of the Turkish party system see Ozbudun (1981:228-240).

[4] These changes are documented empirically by Ozbudun (1979) and Erguder (1981, 1982).

[5] Mardin (1966) provides a good account of the social and cultural roots of oppositionalism and intolerance of criticism which have been traditionally ingrained in Turkish social psychology

and which were manifest in the party system during
the 1950s, undermining its moderation. His analysis provides a plausible explanation of the lack
of accommodation between key actors in what appeared, on the surface at least, to be a classic
two-party system.

  [6] The 1983 results are compounded in their
complexity, not only by their recency, but also by
the presence of a very popular head of the party
which won the election. Ozal's popularity, at the
time of the elections, may be analyzed in terms of
his relationship to pre-1980 parties and leaders
as well as his contribution to successful economic
policies during both the pre- and post-1980 peri-
ods. First, Ozal, while never being closely associated with the Justice Party, served under Suleyman Demirel in a technocratic capacity on several
occasions. He also had close ties to the NSP, as
his brother was one of the influential members of
the party. While flirting with it, he never became a member of the NSP. In terms of former political associations he was occupying a space in
Turkish politics somewhere between the moderate
and more secular right of the JP vintage and the
religious right of the NSP. Secondly, in terms of
policy performance, he was in responsible positions during two important junctures in Turkish
economic history. He was heading the State Planning Organization in 1969, when the Demirel government took important measures to stem the economic crisis of the day. It was then that Ozal
started to build his reputation as an economic
miracle worker. More importantly, Ozal and Demirel are known as the major architects of the con-
troversial but successful--in terms of short-run
economic indicators--January 24th, 1980 measures
to deal with the severe economic crisis and the
triple-digit inflation of the late seventies.

  Demirel was deposed by the military during
the 1980 takeover, but Ozal stayed in power as the
major economic brain behind the policies of the
new military-backed government. The policies were
a continuation of the January 24th measures. He
resigned his post almost a year before the 1983
elections and was not a member of the government
when economic performance appeared to be heading
towards rough water once again.

  [7] The Turkish local elections of March, 1984,

free from many of the restrictions placed on the 1983 national election, provided support for the former, more optimistic interpretation. The Motherland Party repeated its electoral success at the polls, with about 42 percent of the votes. The MP also captured fifty-two mayoral positions out of sixty-seven provincial centers. The other post-1980 parties blessed by the military did poorly at the polls. The Populist Party and the National Democrats did no better than 9 and 7 percent respectively, of the total votes cast. One of the more surprising results of the March, 1984 local elections was the failure of the True Path Party (TPP), specifically organized as a successor to the JP and competing for the first time in a post-1983 election, to make widely expected inroads into the electoral support of the MP. The TPP received about 14 percent of the total votes.

A second but somewhat more expected outcome was the success of the Social Democracy Party (SODEP), with about 24 percent of the votes. SODEP was organized to replace the RPP. It, however, had not received the blessing of the military in the 1983 election. In the 1984 local elections, SODEP seems not only to have taken over fully the mantle of the RPP, but it virtually eclipsed the Populists, who had been allowed by the military to participate in 1983. After March, 1984, only the Motherland Party, among the new "blessed" organizations (i.e., allowed to participate in 1983) appeared to remain as a major force with substantial electoral support.

Chapter III

THE MAY 1984 ELECTIONS IN EGYPT AND THE
QUESTION OF EGYPT'S STABILITY

Richard U. Moench

Introduction: A Victory for Whom?

In May of 1984 Egypt held national elections
to fill the 448 seats of its parliament, the People's Assembly (Maglis al-Sha'ab). These were the
first national elections under Hosni Mubarak's
presidency. To those outside observers interested
in the stability of the Mubarak government and the
strength of its commitment to continue the policies begun by the late President Sadat, that is,
close ties with the United States, commitment to
the peace treaty with Israel, and a liberalized
economy, the election results were received with
considerable satisfaction. Not only did the government party, The National Democratic Party
(NDP), win a substantial majority of the vote (72
percent), it appeared to have done so in an
election more democratic and more honestly conducted than any since the coup of the Free Officers in 1952 began the revolutionary era of rule
of Egypt by Egyptians. Party newspapers operated
without interference. Yet, the only opposition
party to exceed the newly instituted 8 percent
minimum was the New Wafd Party, a party which is,
in general, favorable toward the United States and
the "open door" (*infitah*) policy begun under Sadat.[1]
The parties of the Left failed to secure a single
seat in the Maglis al-Sha'ab, their proportion of
the vote having fallen below the 8 percent minimum.

Did the May elections, then, produce a clear Mubarak mandate, securing the stability of his regime? There is no question that the victory by the government's party was substantial, and the isolation of the Left definitive. In the short run, the May elections appear to have had a stabilizing effect. The opposition was fragmented and frequently occupied with attacks on each other. The Left chose not to boycott and was faced with accepting their defeat. The Right has consolidated but remains moderate in its call for changes, conscious of the warning from government supporters that zealous reform produces high levels of anxiety among investors. But no election may be interpreted without its contexts, nor its results compared to elections elsewhere without interpretation. Viewed at closer range, the above scenario begins to unravel, revealing a paradox wrapped in enigmas.

Most enigmatic of all is the relationship of Mubarak to his ruling National Democratic Party. If the NDP won big in May, was it a victory for Mubarak or for the entrenched Sadatists of that party? Has the election, in other words, increased or decreased the leverage Mubarak has in moving the country according to a plan that may someday be seen neither as a continuation of the Sadat legacy nor as a return to the Nassir legacy, but rather as a Mubarak plan for Egypt's social and economic development?

Paradoxically, after such a resounding victory, both the substance and the strength of the mandate remain unclear. To what extent does a large majority signify popular satisfaction with current conditions and policies? If the approval is apparent rather than real, then the educative aspects of the campaign may be more informative than the election results. If the election was "relatively" democratic and honest, what is it relative to--the 99.9 percent victories engineered for Sadat by his party, or the promises of a clean election that President Mubarak made to the nation? If the election is an unreliable indicator of the popularity of government policies, then what are we to conclude from the fact that the only party not to emphasize in its platform the need for changes was the victorious government party?

An interpretation of these elections must take into account the indifference of a large proportion of Egyptians to the election. The government estimated that 43 percent of all eligible voters voted.[2] But while the rural percentages are very high, where voting represents kin-based solidarity, i.e. *asabiyyah* ties.[3] in urban areas barely one fifth of the registered voters turned out despite the threat of punishment, for voting is mandatory for males eighteen and beyond. The fact that 80 percent of the urban electorate ignored the election (a figure consistent with non-government estimates of previous elections) may be of more significance for the question of stability than the election results. For the major challenge to the government's legitimacy comes not from those who participate in elections, but from those who do not. Of the non-participants, a special threat is represented by those who do not vote because of an Islamic conviction that the secular state and its political process are illegitimate and must be replaced so that an Islamic society may exist.

A final paradox appears if the argument is valid that the short-term stability achieved by the election is at the cost of long-term instability. For even if the New Wafd Party achieves their goal of becoming a national alternative to the government's NDP, it may be doubted that a nation like Egypt can expect stability from a political system in which two parties of the Right claim to represent the spectrum of popular interests.

In the remainder of this chapter, I shall attempt to provide a context to illuminate the election event and the impact it appears to have had thus far in Egypt. This light is not sufficient to penetrate every corner and permit an analysis in which a single scenario dominates. Instead, I consider alternative scenarios whenever the evidence is ambiguous. By the time these words reach print, the reader may already have information making one or another of these versions more credible.

Mubarak's Presidency

Hosni Mubarak, Vice President under Anwar Sadat, became Egypt's third President when President Sadat was assassinated in 1981. An astounded world outside Egypt learned that the man who had received the Nobel Peace prize for Camp David was not the beloved leader of his people struck dead by a fanatic's bullet, but a ruler out of control, whose style of rule had become the object of ridicule; whose dependence on his foreign image for his legitimacy at home had proved perilous; and whose solutions to real problems had been more theatrical than effective. Hosni Mubarak's style was altogether different. He was a man used to listening, to studying every problem in detail, and to staying as much as possible out of the limelight. If the late President Sadat rarely left unsaid whatever was on his mind, this is not true of President Mubarak. Nor is it easy to discover a confidant willing to leak information on Mubarak's intentions. Rather, the situation recalls the story of a journalist encountering Harry Hopkins, at the time a member of the FDR Cabinet, who, queried with "I hear you and the President are very close," is reputed to have responded "He is."

The mass arrests of critics in September 1981 and Sadat's subsequent assassination had resulted in an anxious and concerned Egyptian population waiting for his successor to declare his personal philosophy of rule. Mubarak's early moves as president bespoke a genuine concern to achieve a national reconciliation. But many of his actions were hard to interpret. The President released most of those arrested by the government under Sadat, except for those under indictment for sedition (Islamic militants). He also called an economic conference in which "one hundred flowers bloomed" in the expressed views of economists from across the spectrum. In foreign policy Mubarak made few and only gradual changes [e.g. restoring diplomatic relations within the Soviet Union]. In his domestic policies, his credibility as a leader remained uncertain although his honesty was unchallenged. He began his frequent trips to the United States, gave lip service to the Camp David

agreements, but refused to allow his ambassador to
return to Israel when the Israelis invaded Lebanon, and he welcomed PLO Chairman Yasir Arafat in
Cairo.   Opposition politicians waited for this
leader preaching national reconciliation to declare himself on the question of the institution-
alization of true democratic rights.   But no such
legislative reform ensued.
     Mubarak had become president without a con-
stituency of his own.   The party he headed was the
creation of Anwar Sadat; the government mostly the
appointments of Sadat.   In contrast to the speed
with which Sadat had moved to consolidate his power, the cautious Mubarak refrained from replacing
the Sadatist cabinet he had inherited, offering by
way of explanation his belief that abrupt change
in personnel was a poor means of changing policy.
He had been chosen to be president by his party;
if he turned against the NDP, where could he turn
for support?
     Mubarak was from the start conscious of the
most vulnerable aspect of the Sadat period--the
association of highly placed persons in government
and the National Democratic Party (a distinction
not easily made in practice) with corruption of a
magnitude that stood in relation to the petty
theft usually associated with large public sector
economies as the pyramids in Giza to the mounting
piles of garbage in the streets of Cairo and Alexandria.   So instead of working through the NDP to
strengthen his support in the Maglis al-Sha'ab in
the elections of May 1984, Mubarak chose to make
himself distant from both the government and the
ruling party.   He began to delegate more and more
powers to his Prime Minister Fu'ad Mohieddin, in
contrast to Sadat, who had virtually dispensed
with the services of a prime minister.
     Mubarak's involvement in the elections took
the form of long television speeches to the nation
urging participation in the forthcoming election.
He discouraged the impulse to boycott on the part
of the Left, and promised honest and democratic
elections--a transition to genuine democracy.   The
opposition parties on the Left and Right were giv-
en guarantees that their newspapers could debate
freely the election issues.   He successfully intervened in support of the New Wafd's legal right

to enter the election and in the reduction of the
proposed national minimum from 10 percent to 8
percent in the new election laws. As a result,
campaign rhetoric was notably lacking in attacks
against the person of the President. Even in
post-election disappointment, the bitterness of
the losers was vented against the ruling NDP and
Prime Minister Fu'ad Mohieddin and his government,
not against the President.

It still remains to be seen if the election
increased or decreased Mubarak's leverage with the
members of his government and with the masses.
In managing to disassociate himself from the corrupt Sadatists he may have gained more respect
from the losers who can do him little good, than
from his party colleagues.

The Election and the Need for Change

There is no doubt that the interpretation put
on the results of the May election will depend on
one's evaluation of how good or bad things are in
Egypt today and why. If a growing consensus ex-
ists that Egypt has major societal, economic and
cultural crises, then the recent elections take on
new implications; for it can hardly escape notice
that while all the opposition parties produced
platforms urging major reforms, the ruling party
banked on the status quo.

Egypt since the mid-seventies is a textbook
case of growth without development. That is, the
growth in national income has created a demand
satisfied not by increased production but by increasing imports. The demand itself is not a result of an enlarged productive capacity but of
windfall profits and therefore temporary sources
of income, especially those due to the petroleum
price rises of the 1970s: remittances of Egyptian
workers in Libya and the Gulf, export revenues
from Egyptian petroleum, and pre-boycott Saudi and
Kuwaiti spending in Egypt. Rising imports have
not succeeded in controlling inflation because *infitah* incentives permit unregulated prices. These
same policies have rendered public sector companies less competitive from inadequate financing,
"social" pricing, and unequal competition. The

actual result has been that expensive foreign imports have chased cheap domestic goods off the market, and productivity has diminished. The incentives granted the investment sector by *infitah* laws have resulted in quick-profit enterprise, mainly construction of luxury flats and hotels staffed by foreigners.

Some see the sovereignty of the Egyptian state as hostage to the mounting foreign debt, the servicing of which now requires more than a quarter of the government's total revenues. The large contributers to government revenues are not doing as well as one could hope. Tourism shows a net loss, with more Egyptian expenditures outside Egypt than foreigners' expenditures inside. The Suez canal is a major source of revenue, along with other public sector companies. Foreign capital investment has been disappointing; and foreign aid monies largely return to their origins with the remainder badly distributed among Egyptians.

The agricultural sector's productivity is declining as the result of urban expansion on previously cultivated land, soil drainage problems related to the high dam, and the depletion of the surplus pool of cheap agricultural labor due to the labor demands in urban construction and in the Gulf states. Agricultural laborers can now demand wages in excess of those expected by university graduates. Regulated prices cover some but not all agricultural products, leading to massive evasion tactics in cropping. Regulated land rents, a product of the land reforms of the 1960s, are no longer consistent with land values, so private investment is at a standstill while foreign aid monies mainly go toward mechanization of the larger farms. Farmers who cannot afford either capital intensive production or the price of hired labor are abandoning farming for the service sector. Thus 60 percent of Egypt's basic foods (and 80 percent of her wheat) are now imported.

Education is free but inadequate for the swelling school and university populations. Private instruction as a remedy for declining educational standards is available only to the wealthy. Increasing numbers of teachers moonlight to stay alive. The bourgeoisie's prejudices against polytechnical training for their offspring feeds a la-

54

bor shortage in which plumbers and electricians
make more income than cabinet ministers.

Despite the booming construction industry,
the greatest single problem in urban areas is
housing. While thousands of luxury flats remain
vacant, the estimated number of low-to middle-in-
come units needed is close to three million (Rouleau 1984)a. With a capacity for producing perhaps 200,000 units each year, the solution cannot
catch up with the problem. In addition to housing, all facilities in the major cities--sewers,
water supply, reliable telephone communication,
public transportation, electric power, garbage
collection, parking--are inadequate due to the
staggering rise in urban populations. Crime has
risen, making walking on Cairo streets (the only
reliable mode of transportation) dangerous at certain hours. This unhappy state of affairs makes
Egyptians respond as the cartoon character who,
viewing a typically optimistic newspaper headline
during the last years of Sadat's presidency,
moaned "Not another year of prosperity! I can't
afford it!"

The Maglis al-Sha'ab and Its Powers

The structure of the Egyptian government is
unique, reflecting the styles of Egypt's presi-
dents since 1952. The president is head of state,
head of the government, and head of the ruling
party. President Mubarak's decision to delegate
authority is not typical. The power of the president is not constitutionally balanced by independent judicial and legislative branches. The president appoints the minister of justice as a member
of his cabinet, who presides over the Council of
Justice, which appoints judges. Presidential decrees have the force of law prior to their ratification by the Assembly. Much of Egypt's recent
legislation originated as decrees.

The Maglis al-Sha'ab was never intended as an
autonomous legislative body. When created by Nassir as the National Assembly, its functions were
specifically limited to the ratification of laws
and budgets, the nomination of the president (after which he is elected by a plebiscite), and the

power to question members of the cabinet on policy issues. The president has the power to dissolve the Maglis al-Sha'ab and to appoint its speaker. These prerogatives combined with the overwhelming domination of the Maglis al-Sha'ab by the ruling party have ensured that parliament functions as a rubber stamp, automatically ratifying legislation presented it by the executive branch. In the past, the Maglis al-Sha'ab has performed obediently by disciplining or expelling members who spoke against the president.

Policy advice was, in theory, the province of a second body, the National Union, known as the Arab Socialist Union (ASU) since the Charter of 1962.[4] The ASU was also responsible for the press ---all the major newspapers and magazines having been nationalized under Nassir. The ASU was abolished by Sadat in 1979. To fill this void, especially with respect to the exercise of public ownership and control over the national press Sadat created a second parliamentary body, the Maglis al-Shurah. Its functions in addition to owning the national press, have included occasional advice to the President regarding legislation. The 210 members of the prestigious Maglis al-Shurah are two-thirds elected and one-third appointed by the president. In the last Maglis al-Shurah election in 1980, use of the party list system, winner take all, resulted in a clean sweep for the government's National Democratic Party. Most opposition politicians consider the Maglis al-Shurah to be an expensive frill. The Left party platforms proposed eliminating it altogether, while the Right called for providing it with legislative functions to serve as a kind of "upper house".

The Maglis al-Sha'ab originally consisted of 350 elected parliamentarians supplemented by presidential appointment of up to ten additional members. It grew under President Sadat by the addition of a woman's quota of thirty seats. In an attempt to keep pace with Egypt's rising population the Maglis al-Sha'ab has been further enlarged under Mubarak to its present size of 448 elected members and up to ten presidential appointees. Since the 1960s, the parliamentary elections have included the stipulation that 50 percent of the members must be drawn from the

"class" of peasants and workers. In recent years,
this procedure has been attacked both from the
Left and from the Right. The Leftist politicians
object not to the concept of representation from
the underclasses but to the mockery made of the
categories by the loose definitions applied. A
university president may qualify in the "peasant"
quota if he was born in a rural village. The category of "worker" is as imprecise. Most of the
"worker" deputies are employed by the government
and are members of the government's party. Most
of the "peasant" members are village notables
whose local control was increased by land reform
and their role as heads of government-designed cooperative associations.

Under Sadat, the Maglis al-Sha'ab became a
more important instrument of government despite
its lack of real power. Sadat's liberalization
policies included the promise to carry Egypt from
a rule by men to a rule by law. As a result, the
work load of the Maglis al-Sha'ab increased considerably. New liberalizing laws were passed,
quickly followed by laws to limit the liberalizing
effects of the former. The opposition began referring to the Maglis as the "Theater of Democracy."[5]

Membership in the Maglis al-Sha'ab is not
only a matter of prestige and personal influence.
It provides immunity against prosecution for
crimes unless the body votes to remove this immunity. During the past several years, scandals
have arisen as MPs accused of crimes including
drug smuggling, murder, fraud, and grand larceny
threatened to reveal their colleagues' delicts if
the latter voted to remove immunity.

The New Election System

The new election laws ratified by the Maglis
al-Sha'ab in the summer of 1983 established a proportional representation system in which voters
choose party lists, and parties win seats in proportion to their votes. However, if a party wins
fewer than 8 percent of the vote nationally, it
must forfeit its votes to the front-runner. In
place of the former 175 election districts (each

entitled to two seats in the Maglis al-Sha'ab)
much larger districts were created, subdivided
into voting precincts on the basis of a maximum
population of 500 registered voters. While there
are several thousand precincts, the districts are
few (forty-eight) and very populous. In Upper
Egypt, the geography of voting districts is extensive whereas Cairo is divided into five districts,
and Alexandria into three. The number of seats in
each district varies according to size of the population and ranges from seven to thirteen (usually
supplemented by one additional seat in the women's
quota).

The small parties were confronted with the
necessity of spreading their limited resources
across all the election districts to have any
chance at making the 8 percent minimum vote,
whereas previously they had left areas of party
weakness uncontested. The Tagammu' Party complained of these obstacles and others, and threatened to boycott the election. The Socialist Labor
Party, 'Amal, had hoped to lure the New Wafdists
to join them if the New Wafd was denied legal party status, but the New Wafd emerged a strong competitor. Talk of a combined Tagammu'-'Amal list
was stilled when the government ruled that combined lists were illegal.

Voters finding their favorite candidates
listed far down on a party's list saw little reason to waste their time in voting at all, for the
success of a candidate was a function both of the
strength of his party and the ordering of the
names on the lists. A weak party could expect no
more than the top of the list to be seated, and
the names might be quite unfamiliar to voters in
most of the precincts, given the size of the districts. Some candidates unhappy with their position in the list dropped out of the race.

If President Mubarak's concern with eliminating the corruption in his party is genuine, as
most think, the new election system put into operation for the May 1984 elections is a dubious instrument for furthering his intentions. The new
system gives party leaders more control than before over the selection of candidates and makes it
impossible for individuals to run as independents
or for popular candidates to be elected if they

are associated with weak parties. The new system
of electing party lists was justified by the President as a means for making the May elections an
open debate on issues rather than an assertion of
personal ties; and in the hope that parties would
weed out corrupt candidates in putting together
their lists. But given the limited powers of the
Maglis al-Sha'ab and the dominance of the ruling
NDP party within the Maglis, voting is seen by the
electorate as a means of insuring personal favors,
rather than a means of effecting national issues.
The new system has done nothing, apparently, to
change this perception.

In fact, the opposition party leaders could
be forgiven for seeing in the new election laws a
continuation of the old "theater of democracy."
For although President Mubarak urged national reconciliation and the free and unobstructed participation of opposition parties in the election, his
government challenged the legality of the New Wafd
Party, opposed the participation of a Nassirite
party, and prepared new election laws that effectively excluded participation of the Left in the
new government. The establishment of a national
minimum vote of 8 percent represents a gratuitous
barrier to representation by the Left. A *Rose al-
Yusif* editorial noted with undisguised irony that
no government in Egypt had ever been toppled by
its competition, and that in countries where electoral mimima exist, they are not as high as 8 percent (West Germany's is 5 percent, Israel's 1 percent).

The Most Honest and Democratic Election?

The conduct of the election may have been an
improvement over 1979, but few considered this
significant. Rather, the contrast was between the
high expectations produced by the President's
promise to the nation and the actual procedures.
No one suggested that President Mubarak was in-
sincere in his desire for honest elections. Rather, they questioned his power to control his party. The NDP local precinct bullies were probably
overzealous and unwilling to do less than their
best. Having produced victories of 99.9 percent

in the past, they could well have imagined that their honor was at stake. The opposition parties bitterly condemned the elections as fraudulent. In fact, numerous cases of fraud and the intimidation of voters and party observers were reported. A female candidate of 'Amal was shot to death, and many opposition candidates were beaten in full view of the police, who had orders, apparently, not to intervene. The opposition parties complained that the allocation of television time, sites for campaign speeches, etc. were vastly uneven in favor of the government party, whose newspapers are dailies as opposed to the weekly party papers. The larger voting districts defined by the new election law and the system of voting for party lists rather than individual candidates definitely favored the party with greater access to the media, especially television. Only through the television could voters become acquainted with candidates and their credentials. Nevertheless, the government can be credited with permitting a thorough discussion of the issues in the opposition presses. For example, in October 1983 'Amal's newspaper *al-Sha'ab* printed an opposition manifesto prepared by a committee of opposition party leaders calling themselves the National Committee for the Defense of Democracy. President Mubarak's dissatisfaction with the conduct of the elections may have been behind his prompt replacement of the two top officials (the minister of the interior and minister of local government) who had direct responsibilities for the proceedings. Prime Minister Mohieddin's death directly following the election precluded questions of his responsibility.

History of Egypt's Political Parties

Egypt's political parties date back to the pre-World War I period of British colonialism. The most successful among them during that period were those pursuing nationalist goals rather than the class-oriented parties. The Nationalist Party (*Hizb al-Watani*) was formed in 1907 by Mustafa Kamil, who operated an anti-British newspaper (Beinin 1981:17). His paper's support of labor strikes led to its suppression by press censorship in 1909, afterwhich the nationalist banner was hoisted again but in milder form by the Ummah Party, consisting mainly of large landowners. In 1919 the Wafd Party founded by Sa'ad Zaghlul replaced the Ummah Party as the most influential Egyptian party. By 1922, both Socialist and Communist parties had been established in Egypt but nationalism continued to dominate class interests, and these parties never gained the wide-based popularity that the Wafd enjoyed for over thirty years. At the time of the coup of 1952 by the Free Officers, the Wafd, along with the lesser parties was in decline, having been discredited in the eyes of many Egyptians for its reversal to a pro-palace, pro-British position. When Nassir abolished political parties in the 1950s, there was little support for them and rather widespread support for the notion of revolutionary unity. "Nassir socialism," with its Nehru-inspired antagonism to the idea of class struggle argued in Islamic terms, provided the point of view from which parties were considered divisive. Political parties, suspected of serving foreign interests, were to be in eclipse until 1979.

By the time Anwar Sadat came to power in Egypt in 1971, the country had experienced a demoralizing military defeat, its public sector economy had become stagnant, and a set of liberal reforms instigated by Nassir's March 30 1968 Program had had accomplished little other than to encourage the beginnings of a highly politicized national debate involving progressives of the ASU, students, and the military concerning the liberalizing of Egyptian politics. When Vice President Sadat was chosen to become president after Nassir's death, he insured that the debate on political liberalization continue in the ASU. No force was strong enough to take charge. Anwar Sadat, Vice President of the nation and former? President of the National Assembly was a moderate in the debate and was chosen to succeed as president following Nassir's death.

His immediate problem was the consolidation of his power and the elimination of contenders, most notably leftist Ali Sabri, one-time Vice President under Nassir and speaker in the ASU.

Next he had to react to the growing and increasingly violent agitation for military action to re-
gain the honor Egypt lost in the 1967 war with Israel. The limited October war with its (anticipated) U. S.-mediated cease fire was the result.
Immediately following the cease fire Sadat
launched his policy of *al-infitah al-iqtisad* (open
economy). This underway, he directed the ASU in
1974 to consider political reorganization. The
Liberal Right, notably the newspaper Amin brothers, argued strongly for a return to party politics. This position was also supported by most
professional groups, some university professors,
and even politicians of the far Left. However,
groups claiming to represent peasants, workers,
students, and women opposed a return to party politics on the grounds that it would result in the
foreclosure of gains these constituencies had made
from the "July Revolution". Other opponents included members of the ASU who accurately foresaw
in the recreation of parties a death sentence for
the ASU and the elimination of their own positions
of influence.

Despite this initial hostility toward liberalization, a presidential committee under Sayyid
Mar'ai's leadership proposed the creation three
"platforms" to represent within the ASU the political Left, Right, and Center. The centrist um-
brella organization was to be called the *Hizb al-
Misr* (Egypt Party); the leftist platform was
called *al-Tagammu' al-Watani al-Taqadumi al-Wahdawi*,
(National Progressive Unity Coalition, hereafter
referred to simply as Tagammu'); that of the Right
called *al-Ahrar* (Liberal). The leader of the *Hizb
al-Misr* was the Prime Minister, Mamduh Salim. Tagammu' was led by ex-Free Officer Khalid Mohieddin; Ahrar by another ex-Free Officer, Mustafa Kamal Murad. Although not yet formally "political
parties", the platforms were allowed to run candidates in the 1976 Maglis al-Sha'ab elections. Tagammu' won two seats, Ahrar twelve, the centrist
Misr platform won 280. However, the inappropri-
ateness of this manner of creating political "parties" was indicated by the fact that forty-eight
of the successful contestants had run as independents.

These "platforms" were offically made parties
by the Parties Law of May 1977. But by this time
the end of the Sadat experiment in liberal politics had already been marked by the January food
riots and the government's response. If Egyptians
were increasingly receptive to democracy, the Sadat regime was increasingly hostile to true liberalization, as demonstrated by new decrees, stage-
managed referenda, and the debacle of the 1979
Maglis al-Sha'ab elections. These had been called
after Sadat dissolved the Assembly because fifteen
of its members had opposed the Camp David agreement.

Prior to the 1979 election, Sadat created his
own party, called *al-Hizb al-Watani al-Demuqrati* (National Democratic Party) to replace the *Hizb al-
Misr*. Until this point, the President was supposed to be head of state and not a leader of a
particular party. At the same time, Sadat decided
to create a new party of the Left, since Tagammu'
had from the start acted as an opposition party.
Its newspaper, in its infancy, had run into trou-
ble because of its criticism of the Jerusalem visit and was finally suppressed altogether for
printing an interview with Muhammad Hassanain
Haikal who was, at the time, not permitted to publish in Egypt. So by 1979 Tagammu' was operating
more or less clandestinely; their newspaper *al-A-
hali* a mere mimeographed newsletter handed out on
the streets.

The new party was called *Hizb al-'Amal al-Ishti-
rakiyya* (Socialist Labor Party). To lead it Sadat
chose Ibrahim Shukry, a veteran bureaucrat in both
the Nassir and Sadat administrations and one-time
member of *Misr al-Fatat*, the national socialist
youth organization of the 1940s. Shukry at this
time favored the peace process; and Mustafa Kamal
Murad had even accompanied Sadat on his Jerusalem
trip. In order to assure that the new Labor Party
would gain the required signature of MPs to contest the election, Sadat assigned members of the
NDP to run as Laborites. 'Amal won twenty-nine
seats, but half of these deputies defected back to
their own party. Nonetheless, Shukry and his colleagues became increasingly critical of the Sadat
policies, including Camp David. Moreover, 'Amal's
newspaper *al-Sha'ab* became the mouthpiece for a

growing opposition, including well-known lawyers from the Lawyers' Syndicate whose leadership by 1981 opposed not just Camp David, but also Sadat's decisions to build a tunnel to Sinai, to construct nuclear reactors in the Western Desert, to sell water to Israel, and to allow a foreign developer to construct a kind of Disneyworld at the site of the pyramids in Giza.

In addition to the attacks on the sham democracy of the Sadat administration, the government's weekly journal *al-Ahram al-Iqtisadi* began carrying critical articles against *infitah*. But outside of *al-'Iqtisadi* and an occasional piece in *Rose al-Yusif*, legal restraints reduced the national press to the level of government propaganda. The banner of critical journalism was carried by the opposition press, i.e., *al-Sha'ab*. The President replied on television in long angry tirades.

Finally the issue of corruption in high places was added to criticism of economic and foreign policies. Even the national newspaper editors could no longer suppress news of stagering corruption by officials of the government.

When Mubarak became president, the mood of the country strongly favored a free press which would express the spectrum of political discourse. Mubarak's move to rehabilitate political parties was welcomed by a disenchanted public and provided a first step in making the President's commitment to further democratization credible. The May 1984 elections were to be an essential second step.

Would the Real Sons of the Revolution Please Stand Up?

Of the political parties which participated in May 1984 elections, all but one were in a sense the creation of Anwar Sadat, yet Sadat's name was nowhere visible in the campaign rhetoric. If the visible often remained unnamed, the named was not always visible. Thus an "Ummah" Party was deemed to have satisfied the legal criteria for formal constitution but could find no adherents; while a petition for a Nassirite Party having more than the required popular backing was denied authorization to form, based on the argument that its adherence to the principles of the July Revolution

made it opposed to the new democratic pluralism.
This is an interesting contradiction in view of
the NDP's claim to represent the heritage of the
July Revolution. Although parties based on purely
religious criteria are supposedly banned by law,
the Ummah Party, unlike its earlier namesake which
was nationalist, was conceived of as an Islamic
party.

The Ikhwan al-Muslimiin (Muslim Brotherhood)
has been banned since the 1950s and could not participate as a party. However, its presence was
felt when it joined ranks with the New Wafdists.
The New Wafd battle for legal recognition was supported by the legally recognized Ahrar Party; the
success of the former, however, left the latter
literally a "newspaper in search of a party," as
all its support defected to the New Wafd.

Parties from Left to Right laid claim to the
heritage of the July Revolution, not to mention
the nationalist movements of 1907 and 1919. This
scramble to claim symbols made for confusion and
contradiction: the Right attacked the pan-Arabism
of the Nassirites as anti-nationalist, while the
Left attacked the current dependency on the United
States as counter to the national interest. Most
parties acknowledged support for the continued Islamicization of Egyptian society, while Islamic
associations challenged the legitimacy of the nation-state and its political process. President
Mubarak, having committed himself to a neutral position vis-a-vis inter-party conflict, was highly
visible as the NDP flaunted his photograph on campaign posters; yet the President was never an issue in the campaign debates.

With the legality of the New Wafd cleared by
the courts, the petition for a Nassirite Party
refused, and the Ummah Party ignored by the populace, the number of parties contesting the May
1984 elections was five: two parties of the Left,
the National Progressive Unity Coalition Party
(*Tagammu'*) and the Socialist Labor Party (*'Amal*)
two parties of the Liberal Right, the New Wafd
(*al-Wafd al-Gidid*) and the Liberal Party (*Ahrar*) and
finally, the government's party, the National Democratic Party (Hizb al-Watani al-Demuqrati or simply NDP). None of the five represent a radical
political position. No party of the Left is con-

trolled by class struggle-oriented ideologues,
judging from the campaign rhetoric. Nor have the
family dynasties who monopolized Egyptian politics
before 1952 regained control of any party of the
Right, for these families, while rescued from the
political periphery by the policies of *infitah* and
the return to party politics, were not the real
beneficiaries of *infitah*. The real beneficiaries
are the so-called "parasitic class" of opportu-
nists, without ideological commitment.

Two issues of the campaign separated the opposition from the NDP: democratization and corruption. Two other issues separated the Left from
the Right: economic policy and foreign policy.

The National Democratic Party. The party Sadat
created in 1978 had no innovative program at the
time, and immediately became the party of the government, the ruling party. This is the way it is
regarded today. It is difficult to distinguish
the NDP from the government, or the NDP's platform
from the government's latest five year plan.

As the party of the government with its cadre
of officials and ex-officials, the NDP was not expected to produce surprises in these elections by
way of an innovative platform. Still, there were
two surprises when its platform and party lists
were finally published. The first was that the
platform rhetoric excluded any mention of the party's founder Anwar Sadat, or of Camp David. The
second was that the NDP list of candidates excluded half of the currently seated NDP deputies.

Two possible scenarios have been offered to
explain this purge. The truth may be some mixture
of the two. The first explanation is that the NDP
was merely carrying out the instructions of President Mubarak, who had insisted that NDP members
with the strong odor of corruption be removed from
the candidates' lists. Supporting this interpretation is the exclusion of prominent Sadatists
such as Nabwi Isma'il, former Minister of the Interior, from the list.

According to the second scenario, Prime Minister Fu'ad Mohieddin, as acting head of the party, indulged in some creative pruning of the party
lists to produce candidates more loyal to him than
to either Mubarak or the memory of Sadat. Mohieddin's death directly after the election, while

convincing some Egyptians that divine retribution
was still operative, left this question unre-
solved. In support of such an interpretation is
Mubarak's reaction over the exclusion of Mustaf
al-Khalil and Rif'at Mahgub from the list.
Mahgub, once chairman of the executive council of
the ASU, had been ousted from the Maglis al-Sha'ab
by Sadat for whistle-blowing on corrupt practices
by NDP elites. President Mubarak, utilizing his
special powers as president, appointed Mahgub not
just as a deputy in the Maglis al-Sha'ab but as
presiding officer there!

The NDP platform, as expected, defended *infitah*, but not the *infitah* of Sadat which was a kind
of perverse "import substitution" system (anything
that could be imported was); rather, they claimed
to support a "productive *infitah*," thus hoping to
steal the slogan of the opposition parties of the
Right. NDP campaign criticism of the Left was
predictable. They were portrayed either as Marxists and thus tools of Moscow, or as Nassirites
ready to take the country back to the days when
little democracy prevailed and the government followed policies guaranteed to make everybody poor.
This criticism was also voiced by the New Wafdists. Against the New Wafd, the NDP rhetoric was
more impassioned, possibly indicating grudging
credibility to those writers who welcomed the appearance of the New Wafd on the political scene
with the argument that the "national bourgeoisie"
should have a party representing their interests,
and the New Wafd, with its historical roots, was
such a party (*Rose al-Yusif* 1-9-1984). Members of
the NDP resented the implication that a movement
of the bourgeoisie from the NDP to the New Wafd
would be an exodus of "respectable" Egyptians,
leaving the NDP as the party of the crooks!

'Amal and Tagammu': Parties of the Left. The Tagammu' Party, although formed by the merging of
Nassir Left, Marxists and Islamic socialists, has
enjoyed a stable leadership and a predominantly
etatist politic. 'Amal, by contrast, includes
pro-union elements without socialist ideologies,
democratic socialists, and reformists. There were
in the platforms of Tagammu' and 'Amal parties
many similarities and some basic differences. Tagammu' joined 'Amal in support of democratic re-

forms (long associated with the Liberal opposition of the Right), such as the popular election of the president and vice president, the elimination of the "bad reputation" laws, the separation of powers among the legislative, judicial and executive branches, and the right of political parties to form.[6] 'Amal joined Tagammu' in support of its etatist positions vis-a-vis foreign policy, the economic policies producing dependency, and the protection of the public sector companies from policies aimed at dismantling them. However, 'Amal proposed that unsuccessful public companies be closed down and their workers transferred to going concerns. With implicit recognition that the greatest inefficiency in Egyptian production derives from the lack of worker housing close to their workplace, 'Amal proposed legislation requiring factories to produce worker housing. Tagammu's reforms of the public sector aimed at the elimination of contradictory management and pricing policies. Tagammu's unique suggestion that the government decrease foreign borrowing by substituting domestic savings deposits as a source of capital was matched by 'Amal's unique proposal for reorganizing agriculture on the order of the Chinese village-level brigades. 'Amal's solution to the farmers' complaint over mandatory prices was a purely voluntary cooperative marketing; Tagammu's counterproposal aimed not at eliminating price setting but at more equitable prices, matched with an attempt to deal more equitably with small landlords' complaints that rents fixed under Agrarian Reform in the 1960s, were no longer consistent with land values or revenues. In essence, Tagammu' proposed new land reform policies (Mahmud 'Abdl Fadil, *al-Ahali* 5-9-1984). The parties of the Left agreed in their support for subsidies, but of basic foods only; indirect subsidies such as cement and sugar should be discontinued because they do not result in lower consumer prices (e.g. of housing or soft drinks) but in higher profits for *infitah* companies. Tagammu', however, supported the concept of indirect taxes such as mandatory prices for certain agricultural goods; 'Amal opposed. Both parties sought a return to strict accountability of questionable income comparable to the "Where did you get it?" laws under Nassir.

Both sought the restoration of the public sector companies to economic health, with 'Amal more concerned with questions of efficiency and Tagammu' with social consequences. Although the latter recognized the need for reforms, they were seen as a rationalization of contradictory management and price policies. The Tagammu' Party paper, *al-Ahali*, had adopted the practice of devoting a full page to letters addressing Islamic subjects, many written by fundamentalists; and the party had its share of sheikhs but did not go as far as 'Amal in supporting the Islamicization of Egypt in its platform. 'Amal's platform called for the application of strict interpretations of shari'a including the cessation of production and dispensing of alcoholic beverages (even to foreigners), and the administration of Islamic punishments (*al-Sha'ab* 4-24-1984, Supplement).

Tagammu' looked at the salvation of the Egyptian state as the major political problem; and the only remedies they saw as effective were drastic ones, requiring a period of austerity, an unpopular vision even for those already in power but politically lethal to those aspiring to power. Hence, the great vulnerability of Tagammu' was, as always, its relative unpopularity outside of intellectual circles. 'Amal was less encumbered with difficult choices; whatever benefited the working classes was supported.

Although neither 'Amal nor Tagammu' achieved the 8 percent minimum and thus, elected no members to the Assembly, President Mubarak, empowered by his office to appoint up to ten members, offered to appoint members of 'Amal and Tagammu'. 'Amal's Vice President Helmi Murad was opposed this "handout," but Party Leader Ibrahim Shukry and three others accepted appointments. The Tagammu' leaders agreed to reject offers of appointments. When the Tagammu' member, housing expert Milad Hanna agreed to accept the President's appointment, he was promptly dropped from the party's roster.

Ahrar and The New Wafd: The Opposition Parties of the Right. The Liberal Party (Ahrar) under the leadership of Mustafa Kamal Murad produced a platform that was "liberal" in the Adam Smith sense of economic liberalism, as well as in the Jeffersonian sense of political liberalism which in the U.

S. today is called "conservatism": the idea that the state should interfere as little as possible with the political freedom of the individual.

The Ahrar platform differed in minor respects from that of the New Wafd but was far more explicit and detailed.[7] Since the Ahrar Party won fewer than 1 percent of the votes it is unnecessary to comment at length on its platform. Ahrar's poor showing reflected the fact that Ahrar had been just as Sadat had intended it to be: a faction of the government's loyalists pretending to be in opposition out of courtesy to their president's desire to make the system look democratic. With the appearance of the New Wafd Party, Ahrar became totally redundant. Old pros in the Maglis al-Sha'ab such as Ulfat Kamil left the Ahrar Party and joined the New Wafd under the constraints of the new election law and its 8 percent minimum cutoff.

To what extent is the New Wafd "new"? Its secretary-general, Fu'ad Serag al-Din, had been head of the Wafd Party at the time of it suppression under Nassir. And the "old guard" of former Wafdists were prepared to remind the nation that despite the indignities they suffered as exiles or as the victims of property confiscation and wealth sequestration they were, after all, the pre-1952 leaders of Egyptian politics. One writer compared them to the Bourbon barons who with the return of the monarchy after the French Revolution were willing to pretend that the intervening changes had never taken place and that one should proceed accordingly (Labib 1984).[8]

The early New Wafd campaign rhetoric reflected the influence of the Old Guard. It aimed at stiring up nostalgia for the pre-1952 period and used both the systematic attempts of Sadat to discredit the Nassir's achievements and the recent criticisms of Sadat-era corruption to create aversion to the entire history of the July Revolution.

This attempt was only partly successful. More than half of the Egyptian population was born and educated since the July Revolution of 1952 and these children of the Revolution take the accomplishments of the Revolution for granted. The other faction within the New Wafd is composed of professionals: lawyers, university professors and others, in addition to a new generation of profes-

sionally educated businessmen. It also includes
independent members of the Maglis al-Sha'ab such
as Mumtaz Nassir and some of his colleagues in the
Lawyers' Syndicate, including its president, Muhammad al-Khawaga. These members had no intention
to allow their party to be represented as a reac-
tionary movement back to the days of the monarchy,
but rather defined the New Wafd as a movement for
liberal reforms in both economic and political affairs.

When the New Wafd Party platform emerged it
showed the influence of both the old guard and the
young accommodationist faction. The New Wafd
platform proposed constitutional amendments to
create judicial and legislative reforms. Yet the
stated object of the judicial reform was to expose
the crimes in high places during the Nassir period! The most startling maneuver of the Old Guard
of the New Wafd was their invitation to the Ikhwan
al-Muslimiin to join their party. The Muslim
Brotherhood had been declared illegal after an attempt to assassinate Nassir in 1954, and the current party laws prohibited the formation of a party defined in religious or class terms. The only
common interest critics could conceive of that
would unite the old bourgeoisie with the Ikhwan
sheikhs was their common desire for revenge
against lingering Nassirist influence, stronger by
far than the Ikhwan's rejection of the legitimacy
of a secular state.

Strong doubts about the New Wafd coalition
with Ikhwan were voiced by secularist members of
the party, one of whom (Faraq Fouda) resigned in
protest. Yet the schism between the old guard re-
vivalists and the young pragmatists was probably
deeper. The latter have no desire to fight wars
over issues they were too young to recall. Their
interest, rather, is in building an Egypt that
would safeguard the social gains of the Nassir era
but at the same time rationalize the economy, emphasizing productivity and the free market. The
changes they propose for the economy differ from
Ahrar principally in the fact that the Ahrar platform omitted all reference to the application of
shari'a while New Wafd gave lip service to the
idea presumably out of deference to its Ikhwan
colleagues. Although Ikhwan influence on the New

Wafd platform was barely visible, eight of the fifty-eight successful candidates were Ikhwan.

Summary of Party Platforms. In summary, the Ahrar and New Wafd campaign platforms proposed programs that would make the Egyptian economy into a free-market capitalist economy with minimal interference from government and a dominant role played by foreign investment capital (making *infitah* work), and guaranteeing the social gains of workers through an open political system rather than by government paternalism. The Tagammu' and 'Amal parties proposed programs that would restore the public sector to leadership in the economic development of the nation and restore the economy to Egyptian hands by altering the dependency relationship on the United States and on foreign capital, all in the interests of retrieving the sovereignty of the nation. The first approach openly welcomes multi- national corporations, advocates the internationalization of Egyptian education to provide trained cadres for these firms, and looks on the competition of the world markets as healthy for the improvement of Egyptian production quality. The second notes the deindustrialization of Egypt under infitah to the benefit of a burgeoning service sector which mainly provides services for wealthy Egyptians, Arabs and *khawagahs* (foreigners), and the unchecked consumer demand on a country which is living off its capital (petroleum and remittances from workers in the oil-rich Arab states) instead of directing it into productive investments.

Each of these development strategies has arguments to recommend it, and differences to some extent depend on the relative weight one gives to productive efficiency and wealth distribution respectively. Neither provides a clear answer as to whether democracy is workable in Egypt. The NDP, by contrast, has no philosophical turf to protect but it has organization, appetite, and access to the resources of the state. It needs a controlled press, because the perception of policies which promote rags-to-riches may alternatively result in the hope of the poor instilled by viewing their rich neighbors; or in the resentment of the poor if the gains of the rich are viewed as being at their expense. But only if the economy shows real

growth can one safely dispense with the zero sum
model; and only if distributions are not too dis-
parate can resentment at the disparities be safely
ignored.

Conclusions: Stability, Instability and the May Election

Mubarak's style is so different from his
predecessor, that his strategies are not always
clear. He may have played his cards cleverly,
given the difficulty of constructing a constituency of his own and the divisiveness he inherited.
Still, many have interpreted his remoteness from
the political scene as weakness and questioned
whether he is really in charge. He was unable to
deliver on his promise of an honest election, and
may have hoped for a somewhat larger opposition in
the Maglis al-Sha'ab if he is sincere in favoring
a further democratization of Egypt. On the other
hand, he has made no effort to repeal the emergency laws.

There is no doubt that Egyptians are confused
by all these signals. Many find his behavior in-
consistent with the nature of the system, i.e.,
the constitution invests the president with ex-
traordinary power with which he could rise above
party politics. Instead he chooses to do so by
delegating most of his powers to the government
which is controlled by a single party. Mubarak
has become a symbol of national reconciliation by
abandoning the cause to its enemies.

The May elections, run according to new rules
devised by the NDP succeeded in eliminating from
national debate the proposals concerning economic
policies put forward in the platforms of the Left
parties. Mubarak is not unfamiliar with these
proposals, having heard them expounded at the economic conference he called together soon after becoming president. Some of the proposals, had they
been implemented early in Sadat's presidency,
might have saved Egypt from its present predicament of having to trade its hegemony for wheat.
There is no doubt that the stability of a regime
is affected ultimately by the constraints on its
ability to respond to the needs for correcting
policies that have carried affairs to dangerous

choices. The consumption and import-oriented economy of Egypt is such a case in point. The need now is for drastic measures, and these always imply risks to the stability of a regime. But not to take these risks is probably riskier in the long run.

As for the New Wafd's claim to becoming a "national alternative"--15 percent of the vote as a start is encouraging and perhaps an incentive to an emergent Egyptian business and professional class to support a party favoring a more productive Egypt according to their beliefs in an open market capitalism and a liberal democratic state. Yet the implications of the New Wafd as a "national alternative" to the NDP are not encouraging for the stability of the country. A country of 150,000 millionaires in which a third of the population are in poverty cannot afford a two-party political system in which both parties represent the Right. This does not mean automatically a rising tide of support for a party of the Left, although the popularity of *al-Ahali* speaks for itself. The outspoken advocacy for Westernization by NDP and New Wafd can only produce a more militant reaction among the members of Egypt's Islamic associations. Given the fact that the Left parties and these Islamic associations must draw on the same constituency for popular support, the weakness of the political Left outside of intellectual circles is indirect evidence of the growing strength of the Islamic groups.

Although all of the opposition parties agreed on the need for radical reforms in the system of government, the New Wafd is unlikely, with its fifty-eight MPs to overcome the NDP forces protecting the status quo. Eventually legal reforms are needed if democratization is to be achieved and the bitterness of the masses assuaged. Judging from the worker riots in August protesting the government's "two-price" solution to the subsidies problem, and the new social security arrangements compelling worker's to contribute a greater share, Mubarak evidently sees the times as not favoring greater democratization. Government accused the Tagammu' of fomenting the riots, although the leaders of the striking workers turned out mostly to be members of the NDP.

Despite the fact that the parties advocating democratic reforms did so badly at the polls, this does not mean that the NDP program is popular. Most voters believe that only members of the government party are in a position to offer real patronage to them individually. The new election rules increase the disenchantment with the process; by voting for party lists, a voter is less likely to find someone with whom *wasta* (connections) will work, sitting in the Maglis al-Sha'ab. To the voter, this makes his vote less valuable and his cynicism deeper.

This cynicism extend to the possibility of reform of the system, implying legal changes, constitutional amendments, etc. During the Sadat era, every social crisis resulted in a new law, churned out by the Maglis al-Sha'ab at the instructions of the President. Laws, it became clear, were a substitute for policy, meant to apply to some but not all, and were enforced without regularity (Mohsen 1984). The average Egyptian developed a lack of respect for the law. Power is respected. Liberalization, to the extent that it promises a rule by law, is a farce. Any program which promises new laws to replace old laws can be expected to meet with total indifference.

With one exception: laws derived from a credible moral source merit respect. To most Egyptians, that means the application of shari'a. Thus, the prospect for true democracy in Egypt is contingent on the further Islamicization of the country. This is clearly a contradiction, since it implies that the Coptic population, who, while a minority consider themselves more Egyptian than anyone, would become less partners in Egypt's future than charges of Egypt's Islamic state. Furthermore, it seems reasonable to assert that in the long run, any state defined in terms of religious criteria includes contradictions that are destabilizing.

The influence of Islamic doctrines on the masses supported by the conviction of many intellectuals that it is necessary to treat causes rather than symptoms has left the Egyptian election debates without reference to the problem of population growth. For the parties of the secular Right the greater problem of the moment is the labor shortages caused by migration to the Gulf and Libya and the explosion of *infitah* construction. For the parties of the Left, the economic development of the bottom rungs of society automatically takes care of the problem. Yet all party platforms held proposals for improving education, 'Amal committing itself to a national assault on illiteracy. As long as no one connects these many social problems with the birth rate, Egypt may expect rapidly rising crime rates, deteriorating health conditions, and an aggravated housing crunch that is already of crisis proportions. Egypt's greatest challenge for long term stability could be the education of the Islamic clergy to the belief that a runaway birth rate insures dependency on Islam's enemies.

If the democracy issue at present is a weak one except among law professors and the Westernized bourgeoisie, the election rhetoric of the opposition parties demanding democratic reforms may be quickly forgotten. One-party rule in a de facto sense will undermine the role the May election was supposed to have played in the transition of Sadat's Egypt to a less corrupt, more democratic national effort under a leader who listens to all, parades himself infrequently, and demands a knowledge of the details of problems. The disappointment of the opposition politicians does not make them a threat to the regime. Rather, the great challenge to the regime, other than its inability to cope with the immensity of the problems confronting it, lies in the increasing numbers of Egyptians who have moved from indifference in the political process to the view that the political process itself is not legitimate and must be replaced. Alarmists are already improvising scenarios with Khoumaini-type revolutions or Lebanese-style confessional strife (Rouleau 1984b). The alarmists' fears are based on the conclusion that, in the absence of government-directed, orderly change, changes will occur spontaneously from below. Given the weakness of the political Left, religious fundamentalists have the field to themselves, ultimately producing a Khoumaini-type revolution, or more likely, sectarian strife, Lebanon style. The Liberal Right recognizes the problems as economic, but sees the solution in foreign-aid

fueled development. This reflects a lack of
awareness that a large part of the current dissatisfaction among Egyptians stems from the discrep-
ancy between their expectations of economic bet-
terment and current conditions, especially for
public sector workers and families not receiving
remittances from the Gulf or Libya.

The Mubarak government so far has chosen remedies rather than solutions, in an attempt to pla-
cate both the IMF and student and worker acti-
vists. Violence in the streets thus far has been
episodic and small-scale, but the recent coup in
the Sudan has not passed unnoticed in Cairo. Mubarak was witness to the ill-conceived attempt of
his predecessor to gain legitimacy at home through
a strong positive image abroad. Yet there seems
to be no substitute at the moment for American
aid. Tagammu"s proposed domestic source of capital may be a step in the right direction, but cannot solve Egypt's foreign debt. Given all the economic constraints, it may be, as the NDP contend,
that giving more democratic access to the system
will threaten the stability of the government. It
might also serve to check the mounting disaffection of Egypt's burgeoning student population, in
whose hands Egypt's future must rest.

Postscript

In the year since this chapter was drafted, events in Egypt make predictions of instability obsolete; Egypt has been jolted by violent upheavals, and the Mubarak presidency is under fire from every direction. But the dissatisfaction with his politics is tempered by the ambiguity of his direction and a lack of hostility toward the man. The opposition are concerned that even if he understands Egypt's problems to be economic, he may be too weak to withstand the combined NDP-American-Israeli-IMF pressure to contain, harshly if necessary, overt and vocal opposition. The latter, for their part, fear that Mubarak may lack the strength to move forward with policies close to their interests: "normalization" of relations with Israel, exemption from local laws for American businesses, lifting of subsidies, etc.

Despite the student demonstrations, worker's strikes, the humiliating, bungled rescue of passengers on a hijacked airliner in Malta, the indignity of the Achille Lauro affair which ended with a United States Air Force plane being forced down an Egyptian military plane this past year, President Mubarak's popularity with the Egyptian middle classes may acutally have risen due to his handling of the February security police riots (Seib, *Wall Street Journal* 2-27-1986). In part, this approval is probably due to the unpopularity of these illiterate and badly paid guardians of public order. In part, it is also the product of the unprecedented candor of the Administration's televised coverage of the events. The immediate reaction of most Egyptians (telephone communications from Egypt) appears to have been relief that the response of the Administration was so prompt and firm, that the rioting was contained before it involved civilian masses, and that the army, the instrument of containment, demonstrated exemplary behavior toward civilians in enforcing curfews. On reflection, voices from the Left wondered at the role the army had acquired in the process, while a prominent Wafdist expressed belated astonishment at the stupidity of a policy that assigns recruits from the have-not classes--mistreated and underpaid--to protect the haves and their proper-

ty! The targets for destruction of the police
rioters and their disguised officer-leaders were
nightclubs and luxury hotels located near their
barracks.

President Mubarak's power within his party is
still unclear. The party is fragmented into three
factions. The first, led by Prime Minister Ali
Lutfy, reflects the power base of the Businessmen's Association, a powerful policy making body
in this dependent country. The second faction
backs Field Marshall Abu Ghazala, Minister of Defense. He is considered pro-American and backed
by his senior officers. The third faction is led
by Minister of Agriculture and NDP chairman, Yusif
Wali, whose power with the party's Sadatists in
the Maglis al-Sha'ab is considerable. Thus the
Maglis has been able to reverse almost all of Mubarak's reforms dealing with everything from creative banking practices to outright bilking (*al-
Wafd* 3-1986). According to an NDP minister who
prefers not to be named, the newly elected members
of the People's Assembly are even more corrupt
than their predecessors. Reformist MPs risk liti-
gation after the lifting of their parliamentary
immunity by a two-thirds vote of their colleagues.

Mubarak's apparent helplessness with respect
to economic crises and his apparent insensitivity
to the oppositions's continuous call for further
democratization have produced open verbal confron-
tations with the opposition writers. Since the
Achille Lauro affair, even *al-Wafd* is critical of
Egypt's pro-American policy. *Al-Sha'ab*, under a
new editor, virtually challenges the President to
repent, liberate himself from his party and the
country from United States dependency. *Al-Ahali*
urges him to acknowledge that present policies are
the causes not the solutions to Egypt's social
turmoil. For a brief period, even *al-Ahrar* boasted
a surge in readership under a Nassirite editor!
To his credit, although occasionally *sounding* like
his Sadat, Mubarak has so far not acted like him
by closing down the opposition newspapers and ar-
resting his critics. Indeed, he even allowed edi-
torials in *Akbar al-Yom* by the well-known Nassir-
period journalist, M. Hassanain Haikal. Even more
startling was the fact that the government's organ
al-Ahram was permitted to break the story about

the Reagan Administration's secret attempts to involve Egypt in plans to assassinate Khadafi (*al-Ahram* 3-31-86).

Egypt's economic problems are critical. Tourism, victim of the rash of terrorist actions, is virtually nonexistant. Canal revenues suffer from the same problem. Egypt cut production of petroleum this year, only to find revenues further depleted by disastrously falling oil prices. A contingent of some tens of thousands of Egyptian workers in the Gulf are expected immmanently to repatriate due to falling oil prices. Questions from the press as to what plans the government has made in preparation for the return of all these workers have received no direct answers. It is hard not to find an answer in the "rumor" that the security police recruites' tour of duty was to be extended by an additional year of six dollars a month wages--the "rumor" that is credited with setting off the police riots.

Egyptians are, for the most part, still shaken by the most severe social turbulence the country has experienced since the burning of Cairo in January 1952 and the food riots of January 1977. This uprising was perhaps worse in that it not only gave expression to the serious dissatisfaction with the incredibly inequitable wealth distribution in the country, but it also highlighted the fragility of the regime by pitting the army against the police, with all the deep-seated accumulated resentments between those two groups who who share the task of protecting the sovereignty of the Egyptian state.

Egypt's economic predicament puts Mubarak between an American rock and an opposition hard place. He can hardly afford to reject American aid; but the conditions attached include visible progress with "normalization" which implies restraints on criticism. They may even include military adventures against Libya. They clearly include implementation of the World Bank-IMF stipulations and the continuation of "open door" policies. All of these are unpoplar with the Egyptian masses. The choice between loss of aid and the political consequences of accepting its conditions could be a no-win predicament for Mubarak, depending on the degree of pressure from both

directions. A Mubarak collapse might result in an
Abu Ghazal administration, but its pro-American
orientation could easily result in a coup by militant Islamic junior officers; or Egypt could again
be ruled by an NDP covenant of corrupt plunderers
living off public capital and stifling the voices
of those who object--a scenario for revolutionary
conflict.

Did the 1984 elections play any role in these
recent developments? I see a few obvious and some
tentative linkages: First of all, the election
clearly strengthened the hand of the Sadatists and
allows them to protect their flanks from charges
of corruption through parliamentary maneuvers.
Former Sadat associates, not long ago chased from
the country by the threat of prosecution are now
back and with new confidence. Secondly, the limited success of the Wafd provided an entry for the
Ikhwan into national politics, apparently breath-
ing new life into this nearly moribund organization. Perhaps the election results in the Sudan
will show this to be larger than a single-nation
phenomenon. In any event, since the election, the
Ikhwan members of Wafd have deserted the party in
an attempt to take control of the tiniest parties,
Ummah and Ahrar. The election exposed the con-
trived nature of the political parties, and suggests that further liberalizing the political process would result in at least three opposition
parties of some substance: a Nassirite party of
the moderate Left; an Islamic (revived Ikhwan or
some other); and the Wafd, now without the Ikhwan,
a true bourgeois party. These three would disa-
gree on the value of the July Revolution and the
application of Sharia' law, but they could conceivably allie in their opposition to Egypt's current foreign relations.

The invisible factor in the May elections was
the large number of Egyptians who did not participate despite their legal obligation to vote. Behind this curtain lies a known but unmeasured
force of Islamic militancy. The targets selected
by the security police recruits suggest the possibility of leadership and organization from one of
these apparently not yet unified organizations.
Revolution in Egypt, if it comes, will take a military form but its source will be Islamic. For

these Egyptians, the May 1984 elections will have
been of infinitesimal importance compared with the
United States bombing of Tripoli and perhaps the
Sudanese elections of 1986.

Table 3.1

Maglis al-Sha'ab Election Results

Party	Valid Votes	%	# Seats
National Democratic Party	3,756,359	72.99	391
New Wafd Party	778,131	15.12	58
Socialist Labor Party	364,040	7.02	4*
Progressive Unity Party	214,587	4.17	0
Liberal Party	33,448	0.65	0

Proportion of Electorate Voting: 43 percent

From *al-Ahram* 6-1-1984.

* This figure includes the seats gained from parties
  that failed to make the 8 percent minimum.

Notes

[1] Technically, *"infitah"* refers to the policy changes related to Public Law 43 (1974) and subsequent amendments (Laws 119, 120, 121) which create the framework for a privileged foreign currency sector of the economy, originally aimed at t he introduction of new capital (mostly Arab), new technology (mostly Western) and new life into private sector enterprise. Law 43 created an Investment Authority to screen projects, established priorities for projects, offered investors corporate tax breaks, established free zones, and defined joint foreign-public sector enterprises as legally exempt from restrictions on import/export, labor practices, etc. The law also created the Egyptian International Bank for Trade and Development. In the popular mind *infitah* has come to be connected with corruption in high places, instant fortunes from the plunder of public resources, shops full of imported commodities and the undermining of Egyptian culture. See Moench (1984) for a fuller discussion.

[2] Observers from the opposition challenged this figure as too high, a challenge made credible by outsider observations that certain urban precincts drew less than 10 percent of registered voters (Hendriks 1985:14). Overestimating the total vote makes the 8 percent national minimum a greater obstacle for the small parties.

[3] *Asabiyyah* refers to the solidarity base of obligations from membership in tribe, lineage or family. Upper Egypt's society is more "tribal" than the Delta.

[4] The Arab Socialist Union was Nassir's vision of a political party in a single-party state. Although to Nassir the accountability of his regime was not required to be institutional as long as the daily popular affirmation of the revolution signified a continuing mandate, the existence of the ASU as the political voice of the *people* as distinct from the National Assembly, an organ of the *state*, became more necessary after the 1967 defeat. Thus the March 30 (1968) Program led to reform of the ASU, and aimed at strengthening this body, whose membership reflected through quotas the various constituencies of Egyptian society-- peasants, workers, professional syndicates, university faculties, students, as well as represent-

atives of government (members of the National Assembly).

The new ASU (1968) was organized into five committees chaired by members of the Supreme Executive Committee: political affairs (Sadat); administration (Ali Sabri); internal affairs (Abu al-Nur); economic development (Shuqayr); and culture and information (Dawud). These five chairmen, plus the Minister of the Interior, comprised a General Secretariat of the ASU (Dekmejian 1971:280-282).

According to Dekmejian (1971), the ASU suffered from three weaknesses: (1) it was the creation of, rather than the creator of, the Nassir regime (in contrast to communist parties in the Soviet Union, China, etc.) and thus its legitimacy was weak; (2) it was designed less as a *vanguard* party than as a broad alliance of popular forces, thus it was always subject to internal political conflict; (3) despite the functional distinction made by Nassir between the ASU and the Assembly, there was continual political rivalry between the two. Sadat's more secure power base lay in the Assembly where he was president; in the ASU, he and Hussein Shafi'i represented a right wing against a strong left led by Ali Sabri and Khalid Mohieddin.

When as President of Egypt, Sadat abolished the ASU, recalling Nassir's functional distinction between the Assembly as "state" and the ASU as "people", he renamed the Assembly the "People's Assembly".

[5] An example of Sadat's "rule of law" occurred in the summer of 1981. The Lawyers' Syndicate publicized their criticisms of several of Sadat's policies with banners in front of their headquarters. ABC News discovered the banners and did a film story on the protest. Sadat's anger boiled over and he instructed his Minister of the Interior to take charge. Party loyalists working in the legal departments of government entered the syndicate by force and held new elections. When the new slate of officers congenial toward government policies was declared invalid by the court, new laws were presented for ratification by the Maglis al-Sha'ab that would alter the constitution of the Syndicate to give membership eligibility to all law graduates (most of whom were employed by

the government). The law was ratified after the
assassination of Sadat, contested once more by the
displaced officers of the syndicate, and the new
law once again found unconstitutional.

   6 The expression "bad reputation laws" is
used most often to refer to some combination of
the following: (1) Law #4), the Parties Law of
May 1977 which while it establishes the legal basis for the formation of a multi-party system
guaranteed by the 1971 Constitution, at the same
time empowered a committee of the ruling party to
screen applications; (2) the decree of February
1977, which in response to the January food riots,
outlawed secret organizations and increased the
penalties for strikes and demonstrations to possible life imprisonment at hard labor; (3) Law #33
("To Protect the Interior Front and Establish Social Peace") which followed the May 1978 Referendum, and included articles designed to deny access
to political careers to communists atheists, and
pre-1952 politicians (exempting those associated
with Misr al-Fatat and the Hizb al-Watani, the law
in fact aime specifically at blocking Fu'ad Serag
al-Din's attempt to revive the Wafd Party). Other
articles of the law gave government additional
control over the press and established a special
prosecutor with broad powers and a "Committee of
Seven" within the Maglis al-Shurah to investigate
breaches; (4) The 1979 amendment to the Parties
Law denying the right to form any party whose
charter contains language hostile to the Camp David agreement; (5) Law #95, the "Shame Law ('aib),
so-called because of its resemblance to a law under the monarchy forbidding insulting references
to Palace or officialdom, passed in 1980; (6) Law
#148, the Press Law, reorganizing the national
press as a fourth branch of government subject to
the loyalty provisions; (7) #114 of 1983, The
Election Law amending the 1972 Election Law (#38)
and establishing party list system with the 8 percent minimum.

   7 Their platforms appeared in *al-Ahrar*
5-21-1984 and *al-Wafd* 4-28-1984.

   8 Questioned by *al-Ahrar* (1-9-1984) regarding
his opinion of the accomplishments of the Nassir
regime, Serag al-Din replied "The July 23rd 'movement' caused tremendous changes; but I have grave
doubts about them."

Chapter IV

ISRAEL'S ELEVENTH KNESSET ELECTION

Don Peretz and Sammy Smooha

Preface and Background

Between 1949 and 1984 there have been eleven
elections for members of Israel's parliament or
Knesset. With no written constitution, various
constitutional practices, traditions, and patterns
have emerged to direct the electoral system.
Foremost among these is the formation of a multi-
party democracy in which no single party has yet
won a majority of votes, thus requiring continual
governance by multiparty coalitions. Each of the
eleven Knessets has included ten to fifteen diverse parties or electoral lists. From among these
three principal political trends--labor, orthodox
religious, and right-of-center nationalist--have
dominated the parliament with a gradual movement
toward Knesset domination by labor and the nationalist right.

There are no regional electoral districts in
Israel. All of the country is a single district
and voters throughout choose their ballots from
the same national lists of candidates. The total
number of such lists has reached over thirty at
election time. When casting their ballot, voters
must chose an entire list of candidates; they
cannot subdivide their vote between parties.

Since most voters have little or no say in
placing candidates on the lists of the respective
parties, they vote, not for individual personalities, but for a party's total list of candidates.
Larger parties place as many as one hundred twenty
candidates (the total number of Knesset members)
on their lists, although the number of Knesset

seats received equals approximately the percentage of votes received, for example, if a party obtains 10 percent of the valid votes cast, it usually receives twelve Knesset seats. However, to be seated in parliament, a list must obtain a minimum of 1 percent of the votes. The surplus of votes from parties receiving less than 1 percent is usually divided among the larger factions elected.

From the first election in 1949 until the ninth in 1977, the Labor Alignment (Labor Party plus Mapam) and its predecessors received the largest number of votes, therefore, all government coalitions until 1977 were headed by Labor prime ministers. By the late 1960s Labor's relative strength began to decline as a result of internal difficulties and growing disaffection of the Oriental Jewish voting constituency. The right wing nationalist coalition formed and led by Herut party leader, Menachem Begin began to gain support. In 1973 Begin formed the Likud bloc of nationalist factions which became the chief competitor for the votes of Labor and in the 1977 election Likud surpassed Labor to take over the government with the first coalition which included no Labor ministers.

Israel's Eleventh Knesset Election, 1984

Several trends observed in Israel's ninth and tenth Knesset elections were reinforced by the results of the eleventh. Politics is still dominated by two large blocs, Labor[1] and Likud,[2] although movement to a two-party system was arrested by resurgence of more than a dozen other parties that won Knesset seats. Polarization along ethnic lines which characterized voting in the last two elections is even more pronounced. The electorate continues its movement toward conservatism marked by election of several candidates in small right of center factions and only minor differences on most vital domestic issues in the platforms of Labor and Likud. Fragmentation of the Orthodox religious parties, once the third largest bloc, continues after the setback suffered by the National Religious Party (NRP)[3] in the tenth election.

A major difference was the absence of former Likud leader Menachem Begin, an active participant in all previous elections. After resigning as prime minister in September 1983, Begin withdrew completely from political life and from his place on the Likud Knesset list. Begin's retreat because of health and other personal reasons astonished and disappointed his colleagues, especially since he refused to play any role in the campaign, even refusing to endorse Likud or its candidates.

Begin's disappearance may have been a factor in characterization of the election as "the cleanest...in the country's thirty-six-year history," by Justice Gabriel Bach, chairman of the Central Election Committee, the official body designated to supervise the elections (*Jerusalem Post* 8-1-1984). Before the election, there were dire warnings that it would be the most violent in the country's history, even more violent than that of 1981, a campaign notable for its vehemence. Bach mentioned threats that "The violence of the 1981 elections will seem like child's play compared with this campaign" (*Jerusalem Post* 8-1-1984). The threats were never realized, according to Bach, because Israelis stuck "to their democratic ideals" and the parties voluntarily entered fair practices agreements; and because other campaign workers showed a "remarkable spirit of goodwill towards each other."

Other observers called it Israel's dullest election; indeed it may have been, for no charismatic figure dominated, differences between the programs of the two major parties were minimal, and each seemed to make a conscious effort to avoid confrontation. The Labor Alignment's strategy was aimed at winning votes of disappointed Likud supporters and middle-of-the-road floating voters. Labor de-emphasised attacks on personalities with almost no mention of Begin. Rather it charged Likud with mismanagement and economic failures and called itself the party of hope.

The Likud, on the other hand, made an issue of Alignment leader Shimon Peres' character. Likud leaders recognized how small his personal following was and how extensive pockets of mistrust of him were. Playing on themes that had seemed successful in the past, Likud attempted to portray itself as "the national camp" and the Alignment as the party of privilege, corruption, and dovish extremism, hinting at disloyalty on the part of several Labor notables.

Election Polls

Results of electoral polls were frequently published throughout the campaign. See Table 4.1 for the estimates of two of the principal polling organizations. They seemed to capture more atten- tion than other activities. At times it appeared as though the election was a national lottery rather than a political event to determine Isra- el's future. Election polls were a relatively new phenomenon. The Israeli press began to publish rather unsophisticated results as recently as the seventh Knesset election in 1969. Only three dai- lies gave poll results then, but by 1984 they were standard fare in every newspaper and followed closely, much like racing-sheets among horse race afficionados in the United States and Great Brit- ain. See Weimann (1984).

The relatively large floating vote, which was 13 percent by election eve, made most polls seem far off the mark throughout the campaign. As in the months before the 1981 election, Labor held a steady lead over Likud. Finally, in both elections the gap between Labor and Likud was closed on election day.

In the 1981 election the difference was one seat in Likud's favor; in 1984 Labor led by three (Likud won 37.11 percent of the votes in 1981 and Labor won 36.57; in 1984 Labor won 34.9 percent and Likud 31.9). According to the polls, Likud reached the peak of its popularity during the 1982 invasion of Lebanon, when it could have obtained more than a majority in the Knesset. After the Beirut massacre, polls showed a steady decline for the Likud, reaching a point early in 1984 when La- bor theoretically could have received twenty-four more seats than Likud if an election had been held.[4] See Table 4.2.

Party Infighting

Intraparty squabbles over places on the elec- toral list and factionalization also characterized the 1984 campaign. The first serious rift was Tami party leader Aharon Abuhatzeira's break with the Likud government coalition. After several disagreements over economic and social policies, Tami voted with the Labor opposition for early elections. Tami's three votes led to a sixty-one to fifty-eight majority against the government when the issue came up in the Knesset on March 22, and the election was fixed for July 23, more than a year earlier than required by the country's election law, which calls for elections at least every four years.

There were many disagreements among important factions in both Likud and the Alignment. Many members of the Herut party, the dominant Likud faction, felt that the La'am and Liberal parties were over-represented on the electoral list.[5] Herut, the strongly nationalist party established by Menachem Begin in 1948, perceived the Liberals (former Progressive and General Zionist moderates) and La'am (an outgrowth of Rafi Labor dissidents once led by Ben Gurion) as weak reeds, unable to carry their weight and undeserving of the number of seats allocated to them in the Tenth Knesset. After bitter bargaining, the number of safe Liberal and La'am places, i.e., place high enough on the electoral list to guarantee Knesset seats, was reduced. One editorial writer labeled the Liberals, "the Invisibles...a collection of politicians without a constituency" symbolizing bourgeois values antithetical to the populist rhetoric of Herut (*Jerusalem Post* 6-27-1984).

Also, with Begin gone there was disagreement among the leaders of his Herut party over its top positions. Most obstreperous was ex-general and ex-defense minister Ariel Sharon, demoted to minister without portfolio after the Kahane commission report on the Beirut Sabra and Chatilla massacres.[6] Although Sharon coveted the top position on the Likud list, he was only number five. Yitzhak Shamir, Begin's former foreign minister and replacement as prime minister, was the chosen leader by the party council.

The Labor Alignment was also plagued by divisiveness. Its two principal components, the Mapam and Labor parties, were distant ideologically. Mapam, formerly a Marxist socialist party, had been allocated every seventh place on the Alignment list. To many in the dominant Labor party it appeared to be riding Labor's coattails, like the

Liberals who rode the coattails of Herut in Likud. Many Mapam members had long chafed under Labor party domination and felt that they had made too many compromises in the interest of "Labor unity." Mapam representation in top places on the list was reduced and it remained in the Alignment until after the election when it formed its own separate Knesset delegation to protest the Shamir-Peres national unity government formed in September.

The Alignment faced a far more difficult task than other parties in forming its Knesset list. Its spectrum of clients is much wider than Likud's, including hawks and doves, Marxists and Capitalists, Orientals and Ashkenazis,[7] religious and secular Jews. In forming the list, safe places had to be provided for Mapam, for two former Likud Knesset members who defected to the Alignment, for representatives of the Arab community, the *Kibbutz* (collective settlement) and *Moshav* (agricultural cooperative settlement) movement, and for a minimum number of women. To some observers, the Alignment looked like a political supermarket with all brands of ideology at reasonable prices. One writer described it as a centrist, neo-liberal bloc, with pluralism as the name of the game (*Jerusalem Post* 8-30-1984).

Party Proliferation

Indeed, pluralism was the name of the game when twenty-six electoral lists registered for the election in June. Voter disappointment with Labor and Likud resulted in election of a larger number of tiny factions than in any election since the second in 1951. The loss of ten Knesset seats by the two large blocs showed up in election of five more parties in the eleventh than in the tenth. Thirteen of the twenty-six were new, established since the 1981 election. They included several ethnic factions with new lists representing Jews of Indian and of (Soviet) Georgian origin. NRP women dissatisfied with their lack of influence in the religious party formed EMUNAH (Faith) which they disbanded under pressure from the NRP before the election. Several individuals formerly associated with major parties also formed their own separate lists; these included Lova Eliav's list (he was an ex-Labor Party Secretary-General), Ometz led by Yigal Hurvitz, an ex-Likud finance minister, the Movement for Renewal of a Zionist Society led by the Labor defector Mordechai Ben Porat, and the perennial Flatto Sharon list.[8]

Only two of the twenty-six lists were challenged as not fit to run: Meir Kahane's Kach party, and the new Progressive List for Peace (PLP). Even the Communist-based Democratic Front for Peace and Equality (DFPE) was accepted within the legitimate political spectrum.

Kach was previously on the ballot but had failed to win the 1 percent of votes necessary for a Knesset seat. In this election its slogans and platform seemed shriller than before, arousing apprehension among those who feared the spread of deep social and ethnic divisions. Among the more provocative of Kahane's campaign statements was his promise to rid the country of all Arabs, citizens or not, by force if necessary.

The newly formed PLP was perceived by many mainstream Israelis as subversive because of its call for recognition of and negotiation with the PLO and creation of a Palestinian state in the West Bank and Gaza alongside Israel. While hardly radical in terms of international consensus, overt dealings with the PLO were unacceptable to Israel's mainstream Jewish consensus. The party was led by Haifa lawyer Muhammad Miari, who once belonged to al-Ard, an Arab nationalist group barred from elections by the Supreme Court in 1965, and by retired major-general Matti Peled, now lecturer in Arabic literature at Tel Aviv University and known for his sympathy for, and connections with, the Palestinian national movement.

A series of efforts to ban Kach and PLP were frustrated when the Supreme Court nullified decisions of the Central Election Committee to strike both from the ballot. The Election Committee members opposed Kach because it "advocates racist and anti-democratic principles; openly supports [Jewish] terrorism; fans hatred against various sectors of the population; offends the religious values of the citizenry; and negates in its goals the foundations of Israeli democracy" (*Jerusalem Post* 6-18-1984). The Committee voted against the PLP because it included "subversive elements and

tendencies, key persons on the list were identified with enemies of the State," and because its
principles endanger "the integrity and existence
of the State of Israel, and the preservation of
its uniqueness as a Jewish State...." (*Jerusalem
Post* 6-20-1984). Since 1948 the only other party
banned was al-Ard, but now the judiciary was more
inclined to disregard strictures of the Election
Committee than to create precedents which might
limit political activity in the future.

The publicity gained by Kach and PLP through
efforts to ban them seemed to attract rather than
repel voters. After two previous election failures, Kach broke the 1 percent barrier with nearly
26,000 votes to win Kahane his first Knesset seat.
The PLP scored exceptionally well, to win two
seats with over 38,000 votes.

The Kahane list received media exposure far
exceeding the importance of its 1.2 percent of the
votes. What was significant about his victory was
Kahane's ability to present with great clarity a
fundamental contradiction between democracy and
the Jewish-Zionist character of Israel. Others
were unable to answer questions he raised such as
how to cope with Arab nationalist aspirations,
with Jewish-Arab intermarriage, with equality of
non-Jews and Jews in a Jewish state, and with the
dilemma of integrating the occupied territories
with over a million Arabs. He articulated openly
fears and aspirations of a substantial part of the
population that more "respectable" groups dared
not touch, and conferred legitimacy on militant
zealots in Gush Emunim and Tehiya whose hidden
agenda did not differ greatly from Kahane's. A
poll of Jewish citizens shortly before the
election showed that 15 percent thought that Arabs
in the territories should be expelled; 43.5 percent believed that Arabs could live in Israel but
without citizenship rights including suffrage;
only 15.5 percent were willing to give the Arabs
of the occupied territory equal rights as part of
the State of Israel, and 26 percent agreed to give
them self-determination (Dahaf poll, *Davar*
8-30-1984). Some argue that the positive aspect
of Kahane's election was that it would bring to
the surface these undercurrents of racism and militant nationalism, and force those "respectable"

political circles who favor annexation to confront
the contradictions of their ideology, making it
easier to deal with by direct confrontation in the
Knesset. Kahane's victory did elicit counter reaction among the liberal Knesset members and intellectuals, who began a campaign for legislation
against racist incitation.

A principal cause of party proliferation was
fragmentation of the religious bloc. Traditionally the NRP captured enough votes to become a
smaller third bloc after Likud and Labor. From
the first to the ninth elections the NRP held ten,
eleven or twelve Knesset seats. But the Oriental
Jewish revolt against NRP leadership in 1981
halved its Knesset membership then and led to establishment of Tami as the first Jewish ethnic
party elected to the Knesset in thirty years. By
1984 there was even greater discontent among Orthodox Orientals, resulting in the establishment
of still another religious faction, this time an
offshoot of Agudat Israel called Shas (Sephardi
Torah Guardians). Many Orientals who voted for
Tami in 1981 shifted to Shas or other smaller parties because of disappointment with Abuhatzeira's
conviction for misuse of public funds and Tami's
transformation to a semi-secular group emphasizing
social reforms rather than religious tradition.

Other splits in the orthodox camp were created by sharp personality differences and disagreement over West Bank settlement policies. Morasha,
formed from an NRP faction and Poale Agudat Israel
(Agudat Israel Workers), was established by Orthodox Jews who wanted a more activist settlement
policy in the occupied territories. Thus, the old
Orthodox bloc of NRP and Agudat Israel now found
itself with five parties in the eleventh Knesset
(NRP, four seats; Shas, four; Agudat Israel, two;
Morasha, two; Tami, one). Although the total number of Orthodox Knesset members was about the
same, their strength was so segmented that their
bargaining power was undercut when it came to
forming the new government.

Disappearance of middle-sized blocs made Te-
hiya the third largest party with only five seats.
Formed by dissidents from Begin's Herut movement,
Gush Emunim members and secular members of the
Greater Israel Movement (now greatly reinforced by

ex-Chief of Staff Eitan) who opposed peace concessions to Egypt, Tehiya became the standard bearer
of nationalist militants who wanted unequivocal
annexation of the West Bank and Gaza.

Three parties succeeded because of their
leaders' personal followings: Ezer Weizman's Yahad, Meir Kahane's Kach, and Yigal Hurvitz's Ometz. Weizman did well in the polls before the
election, but the three seats won by his Yahad
were fewer than anticipated. However, Weizman
found himself in an excellent bargaining position
after the election when he merged Yahad with the
Labor party and received a cabinet post. The
merger helped to compensate for Labor's loss of
Mapam and the breakup of the Alignment after formation of the new government.

Shinui (change), the last remnant of the once
powerful Democratic Movement for Change (DMC), increased its representation from two to three
seats, and the Citizens Rights Movement (CRM) tripled its strength from one to three. The two parties were perceived as liberal or left of center
and their platforms differed little. Shinui
backed Labor in forming a national unity government while CRM became a bulwark of the new left of
center opposition. Meir Kahane's one-seat Kach
party was the pariah of the eleventh Knesset, the
faction that all others excoriated. Kach became
even more disreputable than the four-seat DFPE,
formerly the party that the others loved to hate.

Economic Issues

Principal campaign issues in 1984 were the
deterioration of the economy, continued occupation
of southern Lebanon, and Jewish settlement of the
West Bank. Escalating inflation, which reached
400 percent per annum by mid-1984, symbolized the
economic dilemma. Most Israelis were protected to
a large extent against rising prices by the inde-
xation of wages and salaries, bank accounts linked
to the dollar, and other financial schemes, but
even these devices were no longer as successful as
they had been in recent years. Israel's international debt was about $22 billion, higher than
Turkey's and nearly equal to Poland's; 70 percent

was owed to the US government and to world Jewry for personal loans. Only 23 percent was owed to private banks. The country faced a $5 billion balance of payments deficit and rapid depletion of foreign currency reserves. A "red line" of $3 billion in foreign currency reserves had been established, sinking below that was considered dangerous by the country's bankers. By election time in July reserves were some $300 million below the "red line." Low worker productivity by western standards was an overriding problem. One economic analyst pointed out that the average Israeli worker received 47 percent of the American worker's salary, but produced only 31 percent as much. In the US, wages comprised 44 percent of product costs, while in Israel wages were 66 percent (*Jerusalem Post* 7-11, 8-8, 10-15-1984).

The economy was an issue that everyone talked about, but no party acted on. After seven years in power, Likud had failed to implement the most basic of its original promises to lower inflation, decrease the bureaucracy, cut government expenditures, and diminish the number of public sector enterprises. Half of the economy was still in the public sector with 40 percent of the workers employed by the government.[9] In June 1984 Likud introduced special legislation to protect citizen's savings and to increase benefits for service veterans. Even Labor supported these "election economics" measures and they were passed accordingly. Some Likud leaders pressed finance minister Yigal Cohen-Orgad for a modified dollarization scheme, drastic income tax cuts or even abolition of income taxes, but he resisted their importuning. Likud claimed to its credit a 19 percent real increase of government investment in high tech and military industries during the year before elections. This, it asserted, was responsible for national economic growth of 4 to 5 percent (*Jerusalem Post* 6-27, 7-15-1984).

On election eve, Likud's Cohen-Orgad promised to slash defense and welfare budgets and said that he would seek a dramatic inflation cut by freezing wages at the 1982-83 level in a deal with unions. "Free welfare, education and health subsidies" to the wealthy would be terminated. Subsidies on food and other items would be cut, and the tax system reformed. Within the next four years public sector spending would be diminished by 12 percent, he promised.

Labor's economic program was nearly an echo of Likud's. It would introduce legislation to protect savings, to restore public confidence in the stock market, and to mobilize capital for industrial and other "productive" investments. The Labor candidate for finance minister, Gad Ya'acobi, promised "evolutionary not revolutionary" changes to prevent a decline in the standard of living. He would establish fact-finding committees on taxes leading to overhaul of the system. These measures, he hoped, would eliminate the underground which some economists believed constituted a third of the whole economy.

Both parties agreed that major budget cuts were essential, but differed over where to make them. Labor promised to save by withdrawing from Lebanon, by halting establishment of new Jewish settlements in the West Bank, and by cutting "political expenditures," i.e., payments benefiting institutions affiliated with the religious parties. The result of these measures would cut $1 billion from the budget and help reduce inflation to an annual rate of 85 percent within two years, according to Ya'acobi (*Jerusalem Post International Edition* 4-29/5-6-1984; *Jerusalem Post* 6-4, 6-10-1984).

To demonstrate the deleterious effects of Likud's economic policies, the Alignment branch in Jerusalem sold tomatoes at 1977 prices in one of the local markets; the cost was one shekel a kilo (the shekel was worth about a third of a cent when the stunt occurred). This, fumed Likud in its protest to the Election Committee, was a typical example of Labor's unfair campaign tactics.

The only candidate with a straightforward program to rescue the economy was Yigal Hurvitz, known as "Mr. Austerity" since his days as finance minister under Begin before the 1981 election. He accused both major parties of "election economics" and offered as the program of Ometz (The Movement for Economic Recovery) unabashed austerity. In his crusade for economic sanity, he warned that whoever won the election would have to pay the bill for the past three "gluttonous" years during which the country wasted resources in a long "orgy" of spending (*Jerusalem Post* 6-15-1984).

War--Peace Issues

Because of its diverse constituency of hawks and doves, Labor could ill afford to confront Likud seriously on foreign policy and "national" issues such as the war in Lebanon, settlement of the West Bank, and Arab affairs. Recognizing the growing public impatience with the Lebanese occupation, both parties promised to withdraw; Likud when security conditions permitted and Labor within six months. Labor made no promises about uprooting settlements in the West Bank. Rather it pledged to suspend further Jewish settlement in areas heavily inhabited by Arabs and even hinted at further development of already existing settlements in regions that were deemed essential for Israel's security. While not a replica of the Allon plan,[10] the Labor scheme for the West Bank seemed to have the plan in mind. Under no circumstances would Labor return to the 1967 borders, stated its platform, nor would a Palestinian state be tolerated west of the Jordan River. Negotiations with or recognition of the PLO were impossible without a change in the organization's charter calling for the elimination of the Jewish state.

Thrown on the defensive by militant slogans of the Herut youth movement such as, "Labor will return Eretz Israel to the Enemy," and "Labor will bring the PLO to our very borders," the Alignment trod cautiously around nationalist issues and made certain that Labor was not associated with the so-called peace forces (*Jerusalem Post* 6-11-1984). To demonstrate continued loyalty to the military, it opposed conscientious objection to military service in Lebanon, a phenomenon that has been increasing since the 1982 war.

The major weakness of the peace forces was their lack of unified political activity. Leaders of the Peace Now Movement, largest of the various groups advocating dovish policies, were scattered among several parties including the Alignment, Shinui, CRM, PLP, and the Eliav list.

Although nationalist zealots were also scattered through several parties such as Tehiya, Likud, Kach, Morasha, and in some of the other religious parties, they were able to assert themselves more effectively because of backing they received from Likud and Tehiya. While the Alignment included a number of doves, it was unable to articulate dovish policies for the reasons previously stated. After the election, the dovish components of Labor were further weakened by Mapam's withdrawal from the Alignment.

Ethnic Issues

Ethnic issues were much less salient during the campaign than in 1981, but this did not prevent further polarization between Oriental and Ashkenazi Jews on election day. The larger parties increased the number of Oriental Jews in safe positions on their lists; the Alignment even allocated a token slot to former Black Panther leader Saadia Marciano.[11] Despite efforts to achieve appearances of ethnic diversity, election results indicated that both the Alignment and Likud were becoming more ethnically homogenous--Labor, as the party of the Ashkenazim; and Likud, as that of the Oriental Jews. The pattern was even more pronounced among native born Orientals and young Orientals who were recent immigrants. The decrease in economic differentials between Oriental and Ashkenazi Jews seemed to make little difference in voting prefences. Differences in income had shrunk from 35 percent during the 1960's to 19 percent by the early 1980s and possession of household goods had doubled among Orientals during the past two decades. The Oriental birthrate remained higher than that of the Ashkenazim--3.6 and 2.8 respectively--although smaller Oriental families had facilitated upper economic mobility, resulting in greater educational opportunities and more Orientals in professional and technical occupations (*Jerusalem Post* 5-22-1984).

Despite increased economic and political opportunities (thirty-three Orientals were elected in 1984), Orientals still resented what appeared to them the superior or patronizing attitudes of the old elites, best represented by the Alignment and its allies in the Kibbutzim and Labor bureaucracy. They saw Likud as their main channel of social mobility. Was not David Levy, an immigrant laborer from Morocco, the second or third leading candidate for Herut leader? Had not Likud appointed Moshe Levy, a son of Iraqi immigrants, as Israel's first Oriental Chief of Staff?

Although small, the decrease in Oriental votes for Labor was consistent, from 24.6 percent in 1977, to 22.5 percent in 1981, to 21.5 percent in 1984. In contrast, Likud's percentage of Oriental votes increased from 51.1 percent in 1977 to 52.3 percent in 1984.

Orientals who tired of seven years of Likud rule or who were disappointed in Begin's failure to confront the economic disaster facing Israel, moved to the right rather than the left, voting for Tehiya and Kach. The militant right thus doubled its Knesset strength in 1984, from three Tehiya seats in 1981 to five, and one for Kach in 1984. The success of Kahane's Kach party was characterized by one pollster, Hanoch Smith, as "another chapter in the Sephardi voter rebellion that started in the 1977 elections and continued this week when those Sephardi Jews who were dissatisfied with the Likud's performance switched, not to the Alignment, but to anti-Alignment parties such as Kach and Tehiya" (*Jerusalem Post* 7-27-1984).[12]

Kahane was especially strong in small, Oriental-populated development towns such as Beit She'-an, Ofakim, Beit Shemesh, and Dimona, where unemployment rates were highest and economic conditions poorest. In these places Kahane received 3.3 percent of the total vote. In orthodox religious moshavim (small--holder private farms), he received almost as many votes, and in the poorer sectors of Jerusalem he drew 2.7 percent. The vote for his party in larger development towns such as Beersheba, Ashdod, and Ashkelon was a much lower 2 percent, but still nearly double the national total (*Jerusalem Post* 7-27-1984; *Ha-Aretz* 8-1-1984).

The large number of Kahane voters among Orientals made up for his poor showing in cities with veteran European majorities such as Haifa and richer parts of Tel-Aviv, where he did not even clear 0.5 percent. Ironically, Kahane, born in New York, was elected by Oriental Jews, 2.5 percent of whom voted for him. If Oriental Jews had constituted the total Jewish population Kach would have won three Knesset seats instead of one (*Jerusalem Post* 7-27-1984; *Ha-Aretz* 7-1-1984).

The "Oriental Revolt," a characteristic of the 1981 election, was most evident during 1984 within the ultra-religious camp, especially in the surprisingly large showing of the new Shas party. Whereas Tami had been created by Oriental disaffection with NRP in 1981, Shas was an expression of dissent within Agudat Israel. While Shas represented Oriental Jews also (its four Knesset members originated from Morocco, Afghanistan, Iraq, and Yemen), Tami leadership represented Moroccan Jews. Shas leaders shunned Tami because, according to its leader, Rabbi Yitzhak Peretz, Tami lacked "rabbinical guidance" (*Jerusalem Post* 7-13-1984). Although an offshoot of the ultra-orthodox Agudat Israel, Shas attained the spiritual guidance of a former Sephardi chief rabbi rather than from the Aguda rabbinical Council of Torah Sages.[13] The four Knesset seats won by Shas gave it sufficient bargaining power to replace Agudat Israel as a political force and to become part of the national unity coalition after the election.

The Arab Vote

The most startling result of Arab voting was election of two PLP Knesset members. Although not an exclusively Arab party, over 90 percent of its votes came from Arabs and its platform focused on issues of primary concern to them. PLP leader Muhammed Miari demanded reinforcement of the status of Arabic as an official language, a change in Israel's national anthem and symbols, appointment of an Arab High Court judge, elimination of the necessity for military service as a requirement to receive extra National Insurance benefits, and no compulsory military service for Israeli Arabs until peace is achieved (*Jerusalem Post* 8-8-1984).

PLP was seen by Israel's Communist Party (Rakah) as the most dangerous competitor for votes

among Arab youths and nationalists who had traditionally supported the Rakah DFPE list in protest
against Zionist parties (91 percent of DFPE votes
were Arab). In their appeals to growing Palestinian nationalist sentiment in the Arab community,
both parties claimed that they were backed by PLO
Chairman Yassir Arafat. Ironically, it was Matti
Peled and other Jewish members of the PLP who met
Arafat in Tunis, not Arabs on the list. In July
DFPE members also met Arafat in Geneva, where, it
was said, he wished them "success" (*Jerusalem Post*
7-13-1984).

The struggle between PLP and DFPE was intense
and bitter. Miari accused Rakah of a "dirty and
brutal campaign against us" (*Jerusalem Post*
8-8-1984). Rakah predicted that the PLP's Uri Av-
neri, a former dovish Knesset member and maverick
editor, would sell out to the Alignment. Boasting
that its Jewish leader, Meir Wilner, met with the
PLO, Rakah circulated posters proclaiming: "The
Wilner--Arafat Talks Prove an Israeli-Palestinian
Peace is Possible!"

Seven of the twenty-six parties competed for
Arab votes and seven Arabs were elected on lists
of six different parties. Rakah continued in
first place as recipient of the largest number of
Arab votes, but its percentage continued to decrease from nearly 50 percent in 1977, to 37 percent in 1981, to 33 percent in 1984. The Alignment remained in second place with 24 percent, a 5
percent drop since 1981. It appeared that both
Rakah and the Alignment lost Arab votes to the
PLP, which captured a surprising 18 percent in its
first Knesset contest. The four other parties
which competed in the Arab community, receiving
between them about a fifth of the vote, were Ezer
Weizman's Yahad, Shinui, NRP, and Likud. Nearly a
quarter of Yahad's votes were Arab, more than a
tenth of NRP's, and over a sixth of Shinui's. The
47,000 Arab voters for the Alignment provided two
of its Knesset seats with enough votes left over
to help elect an additional Alignment MK. The importance of Arab votes was demonstrated by place-
ment of Arabs or Druzes in safe positions on lists
of the Alignment, Likud, and Shinui (one from the
Labor party, one Mapam, one Likud, one Shinui, in
addition to one PLP, and two DFPE).

Some observers divided Arab votes between the
Zionist and non-Zionist parties, concluding that
the 51 percent received by Rakah and PLP represented anti-Zionist "radicalism." True, the Rakah
and the PLP deviate from the Jewish mainstream on
Arab-Israel issues, but they generally conform
with what might be considered a moderate international consensus, i.e., a two-state solution to
the Arab-Israel conflict, recognition of the PLO
as representative of Palestinians, and establishment of a Palestinian state on the West Bank. Rakah and PLP together represent a sizable bloc
that, were it not Arab nationalist, might be considered for partnership in a coalition government.
But Labor would be reluctant to negotiate with
such a bloc because of perceptions by the Jewish
electorate that non-Zionist, "pro-PLO" parties are
not legitimate candidates for cabinet positions.

An article in the Tel-Aviv monthly, *New Outlook*, observed that the dilemma facing Israel's
Arabs is, "...if they want to expresss a strong
protest against the inequities of the current system that discriminate against them and to express
their clear-cut support for the Palestinian right
to self-determination, their only current options
are to vote for Hadash [DFPE] or the Progressive
list. However, if they want to be taken into account as potential sharers of political power at
the governmental level, and if they want to have a
direct impact on the struggle for primacy between
the Religious--Right and Center--Left blocks in
Israel politics, they have to vote for one of the
Zionist parties" (*New Outlook* August/September
1984:36).

An indication of growing Arab political consciousness was the disappearance of "ethnic" or
"notables" lists. The appearance of the PLP accounted for most of the slight increase on voting
participation from 70 percent in 1981 to 72 percent in 1984. Growing awareness of Arab potential
as a voting bloc forced the Labor party to abandon
its separate "token" Arab factions, to integrate
Arabs on its own list, and to campaign strenuously
in Arab communities. Some of the smaller parties
such as NRP still attempted to cultivate hamula
(clan) ties. Now ideological and personal prefer-
ences are much more important. For the first time

the PLP gave independent-minded Arab voters, who
in the past might have chosen the DFPE or ab-
stained, an opportunity to vote on issues vital to
their community.

Conclusion

Results of the 1984 election once again reaf-
firmed how deeply Israel was divided into two
broad camps, the nationalist-orthodox alliance and
the Labor-center coalition. During the past decade the strength of Likud and its nationalist and
religious allies had become almost equal to that
of the Alignment and its associates such as Yahad,
Shinui, and the CRM. Although the two camps originally represented contrasting visions of Zionism
and/or Israel's destiny, Labor seemed to be moving
to Likud's conservative policies in an attempt to
capture votes of those disaffected with Likud's
performance. The country's multi-party electoral
system encouraged intrabloc party formation and
thus prevented either of the two major parties
from obtaining the Knesset majority essential for
a stable government. Rather, the continuing pattern was formation of multiparty coalitions which
tended to collapse under the burden of demands
placed upon them by the diverse coalition members.
Electoral arrangements encouraged disaffection from the two main parties by facilitating
formation of mini-factions by dissidents who broke
from the parent organizations over personality in-
compatibilities or minor ideological and policy
differences rather than because of major substan-
tive disagreement. Thus maximizing a democratic
process which gives separate representation to
nearly every shade and hue of political and social
distinction proved to be counter-productive in
forming effective and efficient governments.
The near stalemate between Likud and Labor
reawakened public discussion of electoral reform,
an issue that had been raised often in the Knesset
and had been the principal campaign plank of the
once powerful but now defunct DMC. Several proposals were on the agenda. They included raising
the minimum number of votes required for representation in parliament from 1 to 5 percent, a meas-

ure that would eliminate all but three parties from the eleventh Knesset. Another bill devised by Labor's Gad Ya'acobi would establish a system combining electoral districts with proportional representation. Ya'acobi had suggested sixteen districts each with five MK's in addition to forty elected by proportional representation elected from national lists, as in the existing system. National lists would require a larger number of votes for election which would be disadvantageous to smaller parties, encouraging them to unite in larger voting blocs.

Other recommendations to improve the situation included major alterations of the bureaucratic system. A study headed by Hebrew University political scientist Yehezkial Dror asked more authority for the prime minister including power to call new elections, as in the United Kingdom. The study found that state institutions were tending toward "rigidification," even "ossification" in health and welfare services. The quality of the government's machinery, said Dror, was declining, "obsolete and past its prime time." Because of changing cabinet posts from coalition to coalition few ministries could rely on long-term planning and few had working planning units (*Jerusalem Post* 7-6-1984).

Answers to the most important questions facing Israeli society--economic deterioration, Israel--Arab relations, the religious-secular and Oriental-Ashkenazi divisions--were unlikely to be much affected by differences between Likud and Labor. On such issues the policies of both parties were captive to increasing conservative and nationalist sentiments of the country's Jewish population and of international forces beyond the control of any party. Once having overcome differences in personality, how to divide the spoils of office, and minor divergencies in election rhetoric, Likud and Labor established a national unity government which seemed the only way to confront the ideological shadings of Israeli politics. While national unity offers no solution to these dilemmas, it helps make it possible for intelligent leaders to examine the possibilities that they would otherwise be forced to disregard because of partisan bickering.

TABLE 4.1

Estimate of Knesset Seats by Modeen Ezrachi (ME)
and Dahaf (D) 1965-1977

Party	ME March	D early April	ME end April	D early May	D end May	D early June	ME May	ME June	D June	D July 3	ME July 4
Alignment	55	52	53	55	54	52	52	51	54	53	47
Likud	37	41	40	40	42	39	40	36	39	38	37
NRP	5	4	5	4	4	4	4	5	5	4-5	4
Agudat Is.	4	5	4	4	4	5	4	4-3	4	4	3
Shas	--	--	--	--	--	--	--	1	--	--	1
Shinui	2	2	2	2	2	1	2	3	2	1-2	4
CRM	2	1	1	1	1	2	2	2	1	1-2	2
Tami	4	2	3	2	2	3	1	3	1	1-2	2
Tehiya	3	5	4	4	4	5	5	5	5	5	7
Yahad	2	4	3	4	3	4	3	3	3	3-4	3
Morasha	--	--	--	--	--	--	2	1-2	1	1-2	2
Eliav	--	--	--	--	--	--	--	--	--	1	--
Kach	--	--	--	--	--	--	--	--	--	--	1

Adapted from *Maariv* 7-10-1984.

TABLE 4.2

Number of Seats Forecast for Likud and Alignment,
Difference between Them, and Sum of their Votes

Time	Likud	Labor	Difference	Labor & Likud Total
1981 election	48	47	1	95
End July 1981	49	44	5	93
September 1981	51	44	7	95
March 1982	54	44	10	98
Sept. 1982 before Beirut Massacre	64	34	30	98
Sept. 82 after Massacre	60	39	21	99
January 1983	57	39	18	96
March 1983	58	42	16	100
July 1983	50	47	3	97
October 1983	40	54	14	94
December 1983	41	57	16	98
February 1984	37	61	24	98
March 1984	36	51	15	87
June 1984	38	53	15	91
July 1984	37	47	10	84

Adapted from *Ha'Aretz* 7-20-1984.

TABLE 4.3

Ethnic Voting Patterns

Year	Relig. parties	Likud	Tehiya	Align- ment	Allied to Labor	Hurvitz	Weiz- man	Kahane	Oth
A. Oriental Jewish votes for parties in percentages									
1977	17.9	51.1	--	19.6	5.0	--	--	--	6.4
1981	15.7	51.6	1.3	21.2	1.3	1.2	--	--	2.8
1984	15.2	52.2	3.2	19.7	1.8	0.5	1.8	2.5	2.9
B. Ashkenazi Vote for parties in percentages									
1977	12.1	27.25	--	31.9	26.0	--	--	--	2.5
1981	9.8	25.5	3.6	52.3	5.0	2.0	--	--	2.8
1984	9.5	19.3	5.0	50.8	9.0	1.9	2.0	0.4	2.3

C. Oriental Jewish vote for Religions parties in percentages

Year	Total	NRP	Aguda	Morasha	Tami	Shas
1981	15.7	5.2	4.0	1.4*	5.1	--
1984	15.4	3.5	1.0	1.4	3.1	6.4

Adapted from *Jerusalem Post* 8-3-1984.
* Was Poale Agudat Israel in 1981.

TABLE 4.4

Arab Vote for Parties by Percentages

	Alignment	DFPE	Likud	NRP	Shinui	PLP	Yahad	Others
1981	29	37	7	4	4	--	--	17
1984	24	33	4	4	5	18	6	7

Adapted from *Leket*, Nos. 41-42, June-July 1984.
Advisor on Arab Affairs, Prime Minister's Office, Jerusalem.

TABLE 4.5

1984 Election Results

Party or List	#votes 1984	#seats 1984	%vote 1984	#votes 1981	#seats 1981	%vote 1981
Labor Alignment	724074	44	34.9	709075	47	36.57
Likud	661302	41	31.9	718762	48	37.11
Tehiya	83037	5	4.0	44559	3	2.31
NRP	73530	4	3.5	94930	6	4.92
DFPE	69815	4	3.4	65870	4	3.35
Shas	63605	4	3.1			
Shinui	54747	3	2.6	29060	2	1.54
CRM	49698	3	2.4	27123	1	1.44
Yahad(Weizman)	46302	3	2.2			
PLP	38012	2	1.8			
Agudat Israel	36079	2	1.7	71682	4	3.73
Morasha	33287	2	1.6			
Tami	31103	1	1.5	44559	3	2.30
Kach(Kahane)	25901	1	1.2	5128		0.26
Ometz(Hurvitz)	23845	1	1.2	30600	2	1.58
(Ran as Telem--State Renewal List--Dayan in 1981)						
Eliav	15348		0.7			
The Disabled	12329		0.6			
Youth and Aliya(Georgian Jews)	5794		0.3			
Integration-Shilov (Indian Jews)	5499		0.3			
Zionist Renewal(Ben Porat)	5876		0.3			
Independence(Ezra Zohar)	4887		0.2			
Organization for defense of tenants	3195		0.2			
Movement for the Home- land(a flat for ever dischared soldier)	1415		0.1			
Flato Sharon	2430		0.1	10823		0.56
Has-Mas-Movement to Abolish Income Tax	1472		0.1	503		0.03
Amka(Victor Tayar)	733		0.0	460		0.02
TOTAL VOTES	2,023,321			1,937,366		

110

Notes

This chapter is from Don Peretz and Sammy Smooha, "Israel's Eleventh Knesset Election," *The Middle East Journal*, Vol. 39, No. 1 (Winter 1985), pp. 88-103. Reprinted by permission of *The Middle East Journal*.

[1] The Labor alignment, a coalition of the Labor Party and the Mapam Party, lasted from 1968 to 1984 when Mapam broke from the alignment to become an opposition party. Mapam, the left wing in the alignment, opposed the 1984 National Unity Government because it included the right wing Likud.

[2] The Likud bloc, formed in 1973 from several nationalist and right-of-center groups, has been dominated by Menachem Begin's Herut (Freedom) Party, emphasising Israel's territorial unity. Until 1977, Begin was the principal leader of the opposition. Likud acquired the largest number of votes in 1977 and formed the new government. It also won the 1981 election.

[3] Until 1981, the Orthodox bloc included the NRP and the ultra-orthodox Aguda Israel. Since 1981, as a result of splits within the Bloc, five orthodox religious parties have emerged: NRP, Aguda Israel, Tami, Shas, Morasha.

[4] Tami split from the NRP in 1981 in protest against insufficient power held by Oriental Jews in the NRP.

[5] La'am was a nationalist faction formerly associated with Labor.

[6] The Kahane commission was appointed by the Begin government to investigate massacre of Palestinians in the Sabra and Chatilla refugee camps by the Maronite Phalangist militia during the Israeli occupation. The commission held Sharon accountable for permitting the Phalangists to enter the camps.

[7] Ashkenazi Jews are those of European and North American origin.

[8] Flatto Sharon fled France, where he was charged with financial misdealings, in the 1970's, came to Israel and ran for the Knesset to escape extradition. He was elected in 1977 for one term only.

[9] During its seven years in office the Likud sold off only 18 minor state corporations in contrast to the previous Labor governments which sold 54 large enterprises including Zim Shipping and

Haifa Oil Refineries (*Jerusalem Post* 5-21-1984).

[10] The Allon plan called for Jewish settlement in sparsely inhabited areas of the West Bank, mostly along the Jordan River to create a security zone, but no Jewish settlement in the heavily populated Arab regions, except for the Hebron area where Jewish settlements existed before 1948.

[11] The Israeli Black Panther movement was formed during the 1970's by Oriental youths to protest economic and social conditions of their communities.

[12] Sephardi is another term commonly used for Orientals or Jews from Asia and Africa, but its original meaning was those Jews whose ancestors originated in Spain before the expulsion of Jews in 1492.

[13] The Council held ultimate authority for Jews associated with Aguda in all religious matters, or those which the Sages considered religious.

Chapter V

TRIBESMEN AS CITIZENS:
"PRIMORDIAL TIES" AND DEMOCRACY IN
RURAL JORDAN

Linda L. Layne

The nature of political representation in
Jordan has been in the process of continual evolution and transmutation since the Hashemite Kingdom
of Jordan was established with its bicameral parliamentary system in 1946. The Parliamentary by-
elections which were held in Jordan in March 1984
provide some indication of recent trends. The
elections drew wide participation and a great deal
of commentary from the Jordanian public. The overriding issue in this election concerned the role
of tribal political structures in the context of a
democratic representational system. What was at
stake was no less than defining the form of political culture in Jordan.
Three models of inherent or possible structures of political representation were articulated
by Jordan's intelligentsia: 1) "tribalism" ('ashairiah), 2) meritocratic individualism, and 3) party politics.[1] Meritocratic individualism and party
politics were put forward by the intelligentsia as
preferable alternatives to what they believed was
a retrogressive "return to tribalism" in association with the election.[2] Following a brief review
of the history of representational government in
Jordan these intellectual views will be compared
with actual practices of Bedouin using the case of
the Jordan Valley subdistricts of the Balqa Governorate. As we shall see, Bedouin practices share
many elements of the intellectuals' views but differ in several important respects.

113

Representational Government in Jordan

Jordan enjoyed limited participation in representative government under the Ottomans. Following the Young Turk revolt (1908), a House of
Delegates (*Majlis al-Mab'uthan*) was convened in Istanbul in 1908 and 1914.[3] Sheikh Tawfiq al-Majali
of Jordan was elected to both and served as Jordan's sole representative there. The Ottoman government also formed a council for the Villayet of
Syria which included six delegates from Jordan in
the first council and seven in the second (Abu Jaber 1969:221 from Madi and Musa 1959).

The period of Ottoman hegemony over what is
now Jordan ended with World War I, and the Great
Arab Revolt led by Sharif Hussein I of Hijaz.
Sharif Abdullah, son of Sharif Hussein, entered
Jordan in 1921 leading a detachment of Bedouin
troops. The Amirate of Transjordan was established by the British mandatory powers on May 25,
1923 and a British Resident was appointed in Amman
under the authority of the British High Commis-
sioner for Palestine. Jordan was governed without
a constitution for five years.[4] Jordan's first
constitution, promulgated in 1928, provided for
the establishment of a Legislative Council which
included proportional representation of Christian
and Circassian minorities. Nine seats were ac-
corded to non-Bedouin Muslims, two seats to the
Bedouins who were appointed by the Amir, two seats
to the Circassians and three seats to the Christians, each for three-year terms (Abu Jaber
1969:223).[5] This Legislative Council was a power-
less body. No law could be effected without the
approval of both the Amir and the British Resident. A National Conference of 150 notables held
in 1928, 1929, 1930, 1932, and 1933 objected to
the electoral law and the Legislative Council.
Their objections concerning the lack of true legislative and representative functions were expressed in petitions to the Amir and the mandatory
powers and in a letter to the League of Nations.
The first elected Legislative Council was dissolved in 1931 as a result of this opposition. In
all, five councils were elected between 1928-1946.
Nonetheless, chroniclers maintain that during Abdullah's reign (1921-1951) the primary form of

representation was through informal consultations with tribal leaders and other Jordanian notables. He opened his palace every Friday for the notables of the country to come discuss matters and air their views.

In 1946, following the war, Amir Abdullah was recognized as King and Jordan gained its independence. A new Anglo-Jordanian treaty was concluded and a new constitution was promulgated in 1947. This constitution resulted in a new electoral law which provided for the current bicameral parliamentary structure. The parliament (*Majlis al-Umma*) consists of an Upper and Lower House. The Upper House of Parliament (*Majlis al-A'yan*) is primarily ceremonial and appointment to it brings a great deal of prestige and a modest salary. It originally consisted of ten notables who were appointed by the King for a term of eight years. Today it consists of thirty representatives, all over the age of forty who are nominated by the King. As Abu Jaber (1969) has pointed out, the Upper House with its royally-appointed, older notables ensures that a certain level of conservatism is woven into the fabric of the legislature.

The Lower House of Parliament (*Majlis al-Nuwwab*) is filled by means of a general election. The seats in the Jordanian Parliament are allotted in each administrative Governorate on a sectarian basis according to demographic proportions that are fixed by law.[6] The first Lower House had twenty elected members (twelve Muslims, four Christians, two Bedouin and two Circassian/Chechan). Over the years it has been enlarged several times to its current size of sixty seats divided equally between the East and the West Banks of the Jordan.[7]

There have been nine parliamentary elections since its establishment in 1947. The first parliament was dissolved in 1950 to arrange for new elections following the union of the East and the West Banks of the Jordan River. At this time the membership in the Lower House was increased to forty--twenty from each bank. Following King Abdullah's assassination in 1951, his son King Talal ruled for until 1953. During the short reign of King Talal a new constitution was promulgated which made the government responsible to parliament and limited the monarch's authority.[8] It provided for overriding the King's veto and limited his authority not only in foreign affairs by requiring that treaties be ratified by parliament, but also in budgetary and legislative matters.

Throughout the 1950s Jordanian politics were characterized by anti-British, and Arab nationalist fervor. The 1950, 1951 parliamentary elections were dominated by radical political parties. Three opposition parties--the National-Socialist Party, the Ba'th, and the Communist Party--won fourteen of forty seats in 1950 and eighteen in 1951. King Hussein ascended the throne in 1953 and moved decisively to counter the growing anti-regime movement. An emergency law was passed in 1954 which gave the government the right to dissolve political parties. By the 1956 elections only three parties were still legal--the National Socialist Party, the Ba'th, and the Arab Constitutional Party. Nevertheless, the nationalist tendency continued to hold sway. Four other parties participated in the election unmolested (Harris 1958:77). Candidates representing the National Socialists won eleven seats, the Communists three, the Ba'th two, and the Muslim Brothers four seats in the fifth parliament (1956). In 1957 all political parties were legally abolished. No parties were legalized again until 1962, following the election of the seventh parliament, when the King allowed certain political parties to organize.

The last parliament was elected in April 1967, two months before the Six-Day War with Israel which resulted in Israeli occupation of the West Bank of Jordan. Regular elections were not held in 1971 since elections could not be held under Israeli occupation on the West Bank. Parliament was suspended in November 1974 after an Arab League decision taken in Rabat which declared the Palestine Liberation Organization the "sole and legitimate" representative of the Palestinian people.[9] A seventy-five member National Consultative Council was created in 1978 to substitute, in part, for parliament.

Jordan's Parliamentary By-Elections, March 1984

By 1984 only forty-six of the sixty deputies elected in 1967 were still alive and the King feared that deaths would soon preclude assembly of a quorum of forty. On January 9, 1984 after a decade of inactivity the Jordanian parliament was reconvened in response to a royal decree, and a constitutional amendment (article 73) was approved which allowed for the holding of by-elections to fill the fourteen vacant seats--eight from the East Bank and six from the West Bank.

The eight new East Bank members were selected in a general election held in four of the five East Bank governorates on March 12, 1984. (See Map 5.1.)[10] Since elections had not been held for 17 years, this was the first opportunity that Jordanian women had to exercise the right to vote which had been granted them in 1974.[11] It was also the first chance for people 20 to 37 years of age to vote in a national election. A total of 558,581 men and women registered to vote and according to government reports, more than 50 percent of those who registered voted.[12]

One hundred two candidates competed for the eight East Bank seats.[13] The minimum age for candidacy was thirty. Although the constitution does not stipulate whether or not women may run for office, they were not permitted to do so in the 1984 elections. Candidates campaigned by means of newspaper advertisements, posters, printed pamphlets stating their platform, and with cloth banners hung in the streets.

The three most frequently mentioned issues were the liberation of Israeli-occupied Arab land, the enhancement of democratic freedoms, and the development of national industries and agriculture. Candidates differed on the means to be used for the liberation of the occupied territories-- some stressed the need for armed struggle while others suggested that all means including peaceful means should be used. Some specified that all of Palestine should be liberated including the Arab lands occupied in 1948 while others were less adamant. Nevertheless, the majority of campaign statements were concerned with what Stokes (1985) calls "valence issues". Stokes distinguishes be-

tween two types of campaign issues: position issues and valence issues. Position issues are
those which divide the country into at least two
issue positions. Rival candidates differentiate
themselves and compete for the electorate's support by advocating one or another of these positions. In contrast, valence issues are issues
that the entire electorate is likely to support,
such as economic well-being. Popular support is
sought, not in terms of the position candidates
advocate, but by associating themselves as closely
as possible in the public's mind with the desira-
ble goal or condition. Success goes to the con-
testant who is best able to form these bonds or
valences in the public's mind (Stokes 1985:8).
Some examples of the valence issues raised by candidates in the 1984 elections are: To uphold justice. To work hard in bringing the voice of the
people to the authorities. To support the athlet-
ic movement and youth. To support women's rights
and the Jordanian countryside. To support the
Palestinian people (*The Jordan Times* 3-13-1984).
Frequently a single candidate would list a long
series of such issues hoping to win support from
all sectors of society. (See for example, Khair's
campaign flyer, Appendix B) It is therefore not
surprising that the political stances of the candidates were rarely mentioned as having any bear-
ing on people's choice (*The Jordan Times*
3-13-1984).

"Tribalism" and Its Alternatives:
Three Models of Representation

The elections raised an outcry from a segment
of the Jordanian intelligentsia against what they
viewed as a resurgence of "tribalism." "Tribalism" ('ashairiah) is a new word which refers to
the placing of family ties before all other political allegiances and is therefore understood to be
antithetical to loyalty to the State. According
to these intellectuals "tribalism" is regressive--
appropriate only to the time before the nation-
state.

We are not against extended family ties, nor
are we against the family concept, we are not
going to be enemies of family relations nor
the ties of kinship nor marriage relations.
But we are against all of this when it is
used as a ladder upon which one climbs to a
seat as representative or a way to a national
position. As we tour through the towns, villages and cities we see to our amazement evidence of a strange return to a time before
the 1940's. Now in the eighties the times
and the people are different... Tribalism
was appropriate and good at the time of no
state, it was one of the means for peaceful
existence in the absence of a state. But today tribalism is a kind of illness and af-
fliction which eats the fortunes and suste-
nance of the people (al-Rai 3-9-1984).

Another Jordanian critic likened "tribalism"
to the Jahilah period before Islam when people
followed the precept "support your brother whether
he be aggressor or aggressed against." But, he
pointed out, the Prophet Muhammad revolutionized
political life when he added, "support him when he
is right by supporting his cause but support him
when he is wrong by preventing him from committing
injustice." Hence, "tribalism" implies a blind
allegiance toward blood kin regardless of their
personal merit or extenuating circumstances.
    This definition of "tribalism" resonates with
the "tribalism" issue in African anthropological
literature.[14] During the final years of colonial
rule, ethnographic studies began to acknowledge
European presence and to explore the affects that
changes instituted by Europeans were having on
tribal systems.[15] During the colonial era in Africa, tribes had been portrayed as autonomous and
coherent social units, but the moment history was
introduced, the old concept of "tribe" broke down.
A new term, "tribalism," was coined and used as an
omnibus category to discuss any aspect of "tribal"
society and culture when studied in the context of
European contact and in "non-traditional" settings. As a result of its broad definition, contradictory predictions as to the future of "tribalism" were frequent, much as they are in Jordan
today.

In contrast with the predominantly positive portrayal of African tribes during the period of colonial rule, the divisive aspects of tribal political systems have been stressed in the years following independence.[16] Geertz ([1963] 1973) and others saw "primordial attachments" as one of the most serious threats to new nations.[17]

> It is this crystallization of a direct conflict between primordial and civil sentiments--this "longing not to belong to any other group"--that gives to the problem variously called tribalism, parochialism, communalism, and so on, a more ominous and deeply threatening quality than most of the other, also very serious and intractable, problems the new states face (1973:261).

There are a number of serious flaws in this assumption which will be made apparent in our discussion of the case of the Balqa Bedouin. I believe that many of the problems inherent in the "tribalism" concept are the result of an organic model of "tribe".[18] Such models define societies as coherent, internally closed systems, and social development is seen as a unified process occuring in a coordinated way like parts of a growing body. These "unfolding models" treat social change as the progressive emergence of traits that a particular type of society is presumed to have within itself from its inception (Giddens 1979:223). The powerful, pervasive, and alien social forces embodied in the colonial domination of Africa or the modern nation-state of Jordan, situated as it is within the capitalist world system, cannot conceivably be encompassed in such an "organism."
Although as an analytic term "tribalism" obfuscates more than it illuminates, one must distinguish between the term as an analytic construct and its use as an indigenous term. "Tribalism" ('ashairiah) is internal to the Jordanian debate, and cannot therefore, be ignored.

Meritocratic Individualism

Jordan's "tribalism" critics put forward two alternate bases for the definition of political partisanship. One alternative to "tribalism" suggested was the selection of national representatives according to a system of individual merit. Columnist Muasher, one such proponent, expressed his opinion concerning appropriate bases for political affiliation in the following way,

> I wish to see people proud because they are part of a professional organization, not because they are members of a big tribe. I wish to see people proud because of their own personal achievements, not those of their cousins. And above all, I wish to see people proud because they are Jordanians, not only because of their surnames (*The Jordan Times* 1-19-1985).

Another journalist interviewed a number of young voters prior to the election and reported the following complaint.

> This is not democracy in the proper sense of the word. All kinds of men are running for elections, and...they are not presenting themselves on an individualistic level. And therefore, people would vote for a certain man for his name rather than his personal background, education and actual abilities (*The Jordan Times* 12-7-1984).

Meritocratic individualism, like its counterpart "tribalism," contrasts an idealized view of tribal identity based exclusively on ascribed status with an equally idealized view of modern, professional individualistic identity based entirely on achieved status. Both are based on a romanticized view of tribal organization and affiliation.[19] They assume that loyalty to a tribe is "automatic" whereas new loyalties such as those to class, party or professional organizations are thought to be pragmatic.[20] Kamel Abu Jaber, a well known Jordanian political scientist writes,

> Surely it is recognized that belonging and
> loyalty to these and similar groups [such as
> those to labor unions, modern business and
> interest groups, chambers of commerce, teach-
> er's associations] are on more rational bases
> than the earlier loyalty to family clan or
> tribe which used to come about automatically
> (*The Jordan Times* 5-4-1982).

This stance overlooks the importance of achieved
status in the Bedouin system of status ranking and
wrongly assumes that the ascribed status of birth
in a particular Bedouin tribe is immutable.[21]
Those who are calling for more emphasis on
personal qualities and less concern with family
background may be making a bid for increased social mobility and wider opportunities for participation in Jordan's formal political structure. A
survey of the social background of the members of
Jordan's Parliaments and Legislative Councils
shows that access to national elected office has
been highly restricted. There has been a striking
degree of personal and familial continuity, even
in the context of drastic changes in the political
atmosphere over time. For example, members of
only thirty-six families held the approximately
eighty seats in the five Legislative Councils
which were elected between 1928-1946. Since 1947,
the 437 seats in Jordan's nine parliamentary
elections were filled by members of only 183 different families (Abu Jaber 1969:226, 235).[22] Even
the leadership of the left-wing parties--Commu-
nist, Ba'th, and National-Socialists--has been in
the hands of the social, economic and intellectual
elite.

Political Parties

A second Jordanian alternative to "tribalism," although less overtly championed in these
elections, is that of political parties. Although
political parties were the most important form of
political partisanship in Jordan in the 1950s and
early 1960s, they played practically no role in
the 1984 elections.[23] Even the so-called "Islamic
candidates" did not run as members of the Muslim

Brotherhood, the only legal party in Jordan at the time of the election.[24] True, all other parties are banned; but there have been other times when outlawed parties have participated unofficially, such as in the 1956 elections.

What is the reason for the decline in party politics in Jordan? It is difficult to say, but perhaps the most striking indicator is the fact that in the 1950s and 1960s the most popular parties were Arab nationalist parties.[25] The Arab nationalist parties which have survived to the present have proved to have little to offer in the way of a solution to the primary concern of the Jordanian public, namely the Israeli threat and the freeing of the occupied territories including the holy city of Jerusalem. The feeling of ineffectuality among Jordanians was heightened following the Israeli invasion and occupation of Lebanon in June 1982.

These concerns explain in part the success of the so-called "Islamic" candidates who won the seats in the Amman and Irbid Governorates.[26] For even though these men were identified in Jordan as "Islamic," the issue which most obviously distinguished them from other candidates was a more militant position on Palestine and Israel than that put forth by many of their opponents. For instance, Mr. Laith Eshbailat, the victor in Amman, directed his Islamic program towards establishing "a society that is aware of the threats it faces" and objected to the fact that government policies were not consistent with "the state of war that Jordan is passing through." He questioned the value of economic achievements if Jordan is unable to defend them. "The society should be turned into a military apparatus to defend Jordan against the Israeli threat." Eshbailat believes that armed struggle is the only way to liberate Palestine because "Israel does not want peace" and he rejects any solution that does not lead to the liberation of all of Palestine including the Arab lands occupied in 1948 (*The Jordan Times* 3-13-1984).[27]

The fact that political parties were not important in the 1984 elections does not mean that this model of political representation has ceased to exist. It simply reflects the absence of par-

ticular parties which are able to offer convincing
solutions to the problems facing Jordan today.
Given the poor performance of Arab political parties especially since 1967, no existing party
seemed worthy of support.[28] Many Jordanians still
believe in parties abstractly as the preferred
form of political organization and lament the lack
of party politics in Jordan today. Having witnessed their neighbor Lebanon crumble under Israeli aggression not only added to Jordanians' sense
of insecurity but also led to increased admiration
for the path King Hussein has chosen for his country through the morass of Middle Eastern politics.
If there were a government party, I believe it
would have received overwhelming support in these
elections not solely from Jordanians, but also
from many Palestinians. Owing to Jordan's development and prosperity, many Palestinians have acquired an admiration for Hussein and a stake in
the stability his leadership has provided. As
Bailey has put it,

> Palestinian subjects, aware that Israel will
> not readily be destroyed, have begun to look
> forward to a future in Jordan and have ac-
> knowledged that Hussein might be as good a
> ruler as they can get (1984:137).

The Case of the Balqa Bedouin

On election day I observed the voting in
three women's polling stations in the Jordan Valley and visited with Bedouin friends in their
homes. The election behavior of tribesmen and women from the Jordan Valley subdistricts of Balqa
Governorate reveals a model of political representation based on the concept of tribesmen as citizens. This as yet unacknowledged and unexplicated
pattern, while sharing some similarities with the
"tribalism" against which the press raged, differs
from "tribalism" in two very important respects.
First, the Bedouin are not returning to a traditional way of life and form of political organization. New frames of interpretation about what it
means to be a Bedouin tribesman in Jordan today
and how, as such, one ought to behave, what one

can reasonably expect from other tribesmen, from a
tribal sheikh, and from the nation-state are
emerging. Secondly, membership in and allegiance
to a tribe is not contradictory with allegiance to
the State. The Bedouin do not find any contradiction in thinking of themselves as "Jordanian
Bedouin." My observations in Balqa indicate that
the emergent forms of tribal identity are much
less a threat to the State than they are to the
authority of tribal sheikhs.

The Balqa Governorate stretches east from Amman to the Jordan River and the Dead Sea in the
west (Map 5.2). This governorate includes a number of distinct constituencies, most notably: Bedouins, Christians, Palestinians, and Saltis (people from the regional capital of Salt, one of the
oldest towns in Jordan). In the Deir Alla and
South Shuna Subdistricts of the Jordan Valley the
population is made up, for the most part, of recently settled Bedouin tribes. The major tribes
in the Deir Alla Subdistrict are the tribes of the
'Abbad confederation and the Mashalkhah tribes. A
total of 12,000 people registered to vote in the
Deir Alla Subdistrict.[29] The South Shuna Subdistrict, stretching from the Deir Alla Subdistrict
south to the Dead Sea is populated by the 'Adwan
tribe, the self-proclaimed princes of the Valley.
Karamah village, a Palestinian refugee settlement,
made famous by the defeat of the invading Israeli
forces in 1968, is also located in the South Shuna
Subdistrict.[30] About 8,000 people registered in
the South Shuna Subdistrict.

A large Palestinian refugee camp, Moukhaim
al-Baqa'ah, accounted for approximately 15,000
registered voters in the governorate of Balqa.
Balqa also includes a large proportion of Jordan's
small Christian population.[31] They are concentrated in the regional capital, Salt, and in the town
of Fuhais.[32] The largest voting district was the
regional capital Salt, which had some 29,000 registered voters.

There were three vacant seats in the Balqa
Governorate. Eighteen candidates ran for the two
Muslim vacancies in Balqa and nine candidates competed for the single Christian opening there. The
two victors for the Muslim seats in Balqa, Marwan
al-Nimr with 10,762 votes and Zouhair al-Zoqan

with 7,665 votes, won a substantial proportion of their votes from the regional capital, Salt (6,405 and 4,049 respectively). Two candidates representing Bedouin tribes from the Jordan Valley came in third and fourth closely behind al-Zoqan. Jamal Abu Bugar from the 'Abbad confederation came in third with a total of 6,861 votes and the 'Adwan candidate, 'Aakaf al-'Adwan came in fourth with 6,470 votes. Neither of these candidates won more than a few hundred votes in Salt but instead pieced together support from a number of small rural districts.[33]

In Balqa 93,734 individuals registered (49,036 men and 44,698 women). Of these, 48,817 (29,597 men and 19,220 women) or 52 percent voted.[34] According to the Governor of Balqa, the percentage is actually higher. He estimates that if adjustments are made for the people who were registered on family identity cards but were abroad or prohibited from voting because of jobs in the military, security, or police services, 70-80 percent of those present and eligible, exercised their right to vote.

Voting took place in over one hundred state-owned locations in the Balqa Governorate, typically in schools. Men and women voted separately. Each voting station was manned by an election committee of three, one or two police guards, and representatives of the candidates, all of whom were charged with ensuring that the elections were conducted peacefully and fairly.[35]

The candidates' full names were listed in alphabetical order on printed posters mounted on the wall outside of the rooms and above the tables where people voted. The fact that many candidates used the article "al-" before their last name was cited by critics of "tribalism" as a conscious attempt to invoke the reputation and strength of a candidate's entire tribe. The candidates were all listed as Mr. So and So--an obvious effort at egalitarianism in a country where the title "doctor" is consistently used as an honorific for M.D.s and Ph.D.s and bears a good deal of status. Voters had the right to vote for three candidates (two Muslim and one Christian) but were not required to cast all three votes.

Literate voters consulted the list of candidates and then marked their choice/s on a secret
ballot. However, a large percentage of the rural
men and women of voting age are illiterate and so
illiterate voters were asked by the voting committee to state the name of the candidates they wanted. Illiterate voters did not have access to the
printed list of all the candidates and so had to
have made up their minds before entering the voting station. Voters were not allowed to cue each
other.[36] Their choice of candidate/s would be repeated out loud by the voting officials and a completed ballot shown to the voting representatives
of the candidates. While the rationale for this
procedure was to ensure fairness, vocal voting enabled all present, including myself, to hear whom
people were choosing. The repetition of a popular
candidate's name over and over again swelled into
a chorus and may have influenced those waiting to
vote. According to one source, some men with
highschool diplomas pretended that they were illiterate so that they could publicly declare their
vote for the candidate from their tribe. The tone
of voice of individuals who voted for unpopular
candidates proclaimed their independence.

During the election Bedouin men and women
took on an additional set of social roles to the
ones which shape their daily lives: namely those
of voter and candidate. Candidates were, for the
most part, tribal sheikhs whereas the bulk of the
voters were ordinary tribesmen and women. As we
shall see, the interests of candidate-sheikhs and
voter-tribesmen were not identical. The relationships between sheikhs, tribesmen, and the State
that were generated during the elections endowed
those relationships with new meanings.

Sheikhs as Candidates

Four candidates from three Jordan Valley
tribes competed for the two Muslim seats in the
Balqa Governorate.[37] Faiz Zeidan Hamdan al-Masalhah and Jamal Abu Bugar represented the 'Abbad
tribes, Abdl Karim al-Faour represented the Mashalkhah, and 'Aakaf Fahad al-'Adwan represented the
'Adwan. (See Table 5.1 and 5.2 for Balqa election

results from selected areas.) Each of these candidates is a tribal sheikh or the son of a sheikh.
Just as in all previous national elections in Jordan, representatives were drawn from a small number of leading families or tribes.[38] However, in
the past, Bedouin representatives tended to be
paramount sheikhs (*sheikh al-mashayouk*, literally
sheikh of sheikhs). Paramount sheikhs were the
recognized leaders and spokespersons for a tribe
(*qabilah*) or a tribal confederation.[39] In the last
few decades the structural range of tribal authority has been shrinking. As the last generation of
paramount sheikhs dies, tribes are refusing to
grant legitimate authority to would-be replace-
ments at the same structural level, i.e., at the
level of a qabilah. Sheikhly authority now rests
instead at the unit of an (*'ashirah*), or clan.[40]
Meanwhile, the King has taken over the role of
"sheikh of sheikhs". This process of tribal fragmentation explains, to a large extent, the difficulty the Jordan Valley tribes had in agreeing on
a single candidate to represent them and consequently why none of their candidates won.
    The 'Adwan tribe had difficulty in deciding
who would run from their tribe in the election.
The choice between one of two possible candidates
was hotly debated up until the last minute. Once
the choice was made, the whole tribe did not lend
its support to the selected candidate. Supporters
of the alternate candidate abrogated alliances
they had forged for this election with neighboring
tribes from the Deir Alla Subdistrict when they
learned that their favored was not to run, thus
releasing these neighboring tribes from their obligation to vote for the 'Adwan candidate. In the
end the 'Adwan candidate, 'Aakaf al-'Adwan, won a
meager twelve votes in the entire Deir Alla Subdistrict.[41]
    Segmentary solidarity does not necessarily
lead to mass support for members of one's agnatic
group. It is entirely possible that members of a
tribe or village feel that their communal image is
better served by voting for candidates other than
those from their group. There are many alternative rationale which can be used to justify not
voting for one's kinsmen, all of which present the
individual as belonging to a morally superior com-

munity.[42] An example of this can be seen with one of the 'Abbadi candidates. The 'Abbadis could not reach a consensus on one candidate to represent them so two ran for office. One candidate, Faiz Zeidan, the son of Zeidan al-Masalhah sheikh of the Masalhah, was considered to be anti-Hussein. For many 'Abbadis this forced a choice between their loyalty for a member of their tribal confederation and loyalty to their King. The upshot is evident in the election results. Faiz Zeidan finished eleventh out of eighteen candidates with a total of 2,827 votes.

Neither did the other 'Abbadi candidate, Jamal Abu Bugar, have the complete support of the 'Abbad tribes. At least one other 'Abbad tribe refused to support him because they felt that it was their "turn" to have one of their members run for office. Nevertheless, Abu Bugar finished third in the election missing a seat by only 804 votes.

Among the Mashalkhah, tribal authority is generally considered to be stronger, more intact, than amongst the 'Abbad, mostly due to the strength and long life of their paramount sheikh Ahmad Muhammad al-Naim who died in 1981. The fact that the Mashalkhah tribes were able to agree on a single tribal candidate and had well organized and smoothly run elections in their territory were indications of the relative strength of tribal authority there. The Mashalkhah candidate Abdl Karim al-Faour received overwhelming support from his tribe. He came in seventh over all with a total of 4,885 votes, nearly all of which came from his home subdistrict, Deir Alla.

Although, as we have seen, there was frequently disagreement about which sheikh should run, there was no mention among tribesmen that people other than sheikhs should have run. Sheikhs still function as a public emblem (*wajhah*, literally face) for their tribes and embody values which the tribe holds dear and by which tribesmen and women identify themselves as Bedouin despite the fact that the political power and authority of sheikhs is diminishing. Tribal sheikhs are not only losing authority over members of their tribes but concommitantly vis a vis the State as the following incident illustrates. When I arrived at a

women's voting station in the afternoon this story
was told to me. In the morning the sheikh of the
village had come there and accused the voting committee of cheating. None of my informants offered
an opinion as to the basis or accuracy of this accusation. Of more importance to them was the power struggle which ensued. The head of the committee, i.e., a representative of the State, would
not suffer such an accusation and asked the sheikh
to leave the premises. The sheikh was appalled
and yelled "ana sheikh, ana sheikh", "I am the
sheikh here!" Two elements of this event shocked
my informants: 1) that anyone would attempt to
evict a sheikh from his own territory and, 2) that
a sheikh would feel it necessary to proclaim his
status, exceedingly unsheikh-like behavior. This
incident poignantly revealed the winds of change
to all who observed. To have one's tribal sheikh
publicly put in his place on what the sheikh considered to be his own tribal territory but which
was more convincingly defined as a state-owned and
operated institution, was unsettling and disturb-
ing to those who looked on. Although the social
role of sheikhs is being transformed, many of the
traditional rules of etiquette about how one ought
to treat a sheikh maintain their moral force.

Tribesmen as Citizens

Voting for a member of one's own tribe is
considered natural and normal. For instance, when
Mashalkhah members living in the 'Abbadi village
of Mu'addi voted for the Mashalkhah candidate, al-
Faour, no one was surprised and no effort was made
to get them to vote for 'Abbadi candidates. But
voting for a member of one's own tribe is not "automatic" nor a "given of social existence" as
those who object to "tribalism" believe. On several occasions the Bedouin of the Jordan Valley
chose to support candidates other than those from
their tribe.

In Mu'addi, a predominantly 'Abbadi village,
the votes were split. The 'Abbadis did not vote
as a tribe. As mentioned above, one of the 'Abbad
candidates was considered to be anti-regime. When
the 'Abbadis were forced to choose between their

loyalty for a member of their tribal confederation and loyalty to their King the majority opted for the King. The other 'Abbad candidate lost 'Abbadi votes because of a lack of consensus within the confederation about who should represent the confederation in this national election. In fact, the Christian candidate Jamal al-Sha'ar seemed to receive more support in Mu'addi than either of the 'Abbadi candidates. Women explained that the reason they voted for Dr. al-Sha'ar was because he delivered their babies in the 1950s. This support was a matter of personal choice rather than due to a tribe-wide agreement.[43]

Another example comes from Kreimah village which is located in the northern third of the Jordan Valley in the Irbid Governorate. There, even though a local tribesman, Basheer Ghazawia, was competing for the one open seat in the Irbid Governorate, most of the women I observed voted instead for the "Islamic" candidate. When the results were tallied, the "Islamic" candidate had won and Ghazawia came in third.

The word for vote in Arabic (*sot*) literally means voice. What are voters voicing? Not simply their choice of a person to represent them in parliament but their identity as tribesmen and as citizens in a modern nation-state. To have a member of one's tribe running for office means that one is part of a politically significant group. It means that one counts. Similarly, to be acquainted with a political personality reflects status on oneself. But at the same time, to be a citizen of Jordan and by that fact, to have the right to vote, also means one has personal and political significance. This was particularly salient to women in a culture where their opinion on matters of national politics had never before been sought and where their word legally has carried only half the weight of men's. Because voting is, among other things, an act of self-definition, tribesmen and women would not allow anyone including their sheikhs to tell them how to vote.[44]

Since the entire electorate in each district votes for both Christian and Muslim members, candidates try to form alliances with other candidates (both Christian and Muslim) and with other tribal leaders. The electoral process thus en-

courages the cross-cutting of sectarian and tribal
ties. However, this system rests upon the ability
of tribal leaders to speak on behalf of their
tribe and ultimately to deliver votes. One sheikh
apparently promised the votes of his tribe not to
one, but to several opposing candidates. The candidates assumed that he could speak on behalf of
his tribe and were purportedly willing to pay for
his promise of support. One must assume that the
sheikh believed that he could control the votes of
his tribesmen and would be able to direct them to
vote for one of the several candidates with whom
he had made alliances. But on election day it was
clear that the people of his tribe were voting for
whomever they chose. None of the candidates who
had bargained for support from this tribe received
the support that had been promised them by the
sheikh.

One of the candidate's sisters had flown over
from Cincinnatti to help her brother with the
election and was stationed as his representative
in one of the women's voting stations in the Valley. She was busy introducing herself to the women waiting to vote and campaigning for her brother. Although women occasionally cast one of their
three votes for her brother, she was exasperated
that her attempts to drill her brother's name into
the women's heads were not more successful and
condescendingly attributed her difficulty to the
fact that "the women could not remember." My impression was that women took great pride in their
right to vote and were voting for whom and *only*
for whom they chose.

Another example of the Bedouin's tenacious
claim to their right as citizens to express themselves by voting freely in this election occurred
in another village when a tribesman who had campaigned seriously for several weeks before the
election for a Christian candidate stood outside
the women's polling place in his village telling
women how to vote. He assumed that he had the
right to tell the women from his tribe (and perhaps the men too) how to vote. I do not know
whether he believed that they would do as he told
them but he certainly believed that telling women
from his tribe how to vote was acceptable behavior. Not all of the women of his tribe agreed.
For example, when a freed slave of the tribe, a

school teacher, arrived with her mother at the
polling station he instructed them to vote for
three particular individuals (the two candidates
from ther tribe and the Christian candidate he
supported). The young woman was offended at the
thought that he would try to tell her how to vote.
She told him that she had already made up her mind
to vote for two of the candidates he recommended
but as for the third, the anti-regime candidate
from her tribe, she said, "we'll see" in a tone
which indicated that she obviously had no intention of voting for him. She told me afterwards
that she did not vote for him but voted for someone else instead.

Tribes, "Tribalism," and Democracy: Implications for the Future

Parliamentary democracy is a western system
of government which was implanted in Jordan by the
British at the time of its establishment as an independent nation-state. The nation has had to
adapt to dramatic social, demographic and political changes within Jordan and throughout the region and each of these factors of change has had
an impact on the people of Jordan, their political
system, and their models of political representation. The 1984 parliamentary by-elections illuminate a number of the current trends.

Political parties were not important in the
1984 parliamentary elections. Nevertheless, I believe that this is still an important model of political representation in Jordan, for Jordan's
Bedouin as well as the intelligentsia.[45] The programs of the Iraqi Ba'th, Syrian Ba'th, and Communist parties may no longer seem suited to the particular political problems which face Jordan, but
new parties which more directly address the Jordanian population may evolve. Rather than singling
out the Bedouin and blaming the lack of party politics in this election on a "return to tribalism,"
one must see the Bedouin's voting behavior in the
context of the nationwide disillusionment with
Arab political parties.

A concern with the personal characteristics
of national representatives may continue to play

an increasingly important role in the selection of
candidates for national office. However, the pro-
popents of meritocratic individualism are incor-
rect when they contrast their ideals with "tribalism." Personal qualities played a role in
selecting tribal candidates in this and previous
elections. Sheikhdom is not rigidly defined and
automatically inherited. Noble birth is only one
of the criteria for Bedouin leadership. Personal
characteristics such as bravery, generosity, char-
isma, and leadership abilities have always been
important attributes of a sheikh. These very
characteristics may be the same ones required of
members of parliament. In addition, some new attributes such as increasingly higher levels of
formal education may be considered necessary.
Those who seek wider access to national political
office may succeed in garnering support from some
sectors of Jordanian society, but among the Bedouin tribes sheikhs are and may continue to be
considered the most appropriate representatives of
their tribe to the nation. Even though a number
of things (such as the inability to agree on a
single tribal candidate, sheikhs' inability to deliver votes to other sheikhs with whom they made
alliances, and refusal of tribesmen to replace
paramount sheikhs as they pass away) point to a
decline in the authority of tribal sheikhs, they
remain powerful symbols of their tribes to their
tribes.

The Jordanian parliamentary elections described in this chapter provided an important context in which to observe the complex interelation-
ships between the various levels of collective
identity that pertain to the Bedouin of Jordan.
The Bedouin's electoral choices were acts of assertion of both individual and collective identity; symbols simultaneously of personal independence and communal and regional solidarity.

The Jordanian concept *'ashairiah* is rooted in
both internal and international political discourse. I believe that the Jordanian intelligentsia's slam against "tribalism" reflects their desire to adopt a collective image which is morally
respectable according to Western criteria. The
resultant portrayal of tribal life in Jordan as a
divisive and out-dated remnant which is holding

the country back (just as the vision of it as an idealized past--symbol of a heroic age and noble heritage),[46] is essentializing and, as we have seen, misleading when applied to real, living communities in the process of recreating themselves in a changing world.

Jordan's intellectuals were correct in the fact that tribal affiliation played a central role in the 1984 parliamentary by-elections. But there was no "return to tribalism." The case of the Balqa Bedouin has provided a vivid example of the dialogical processes by which the Bedouin of Jordan continue to make themselves in a dramatically changed world.

New definitions are emerging about what it means to be a tribesman in Jordan today. For example, although the Bedouin of the Jordan Valley maintain an identity as Bedouin, the meaning of such an identity has changed and includes many new elements such as a more limited role for sheikhs and new sources of nationally-based political status and legitimacy.[47] These new definitions of tribal identity are not contradictory with citizenship and do not pose a threat to Jordan. Tribal identity and citizenship are two complementary cultural forms which give value and significance to the lives of a large portion of the Jordanian population (including non-Bedouin tribally-organized urban groups in addition to the Bedouin). Tribal identity is drawn from an indigenous way of life--local mores, established institutions, and common experience and as such has a certain psychological force. Citizenship, on the other hand, permits a less socially isolating reality and offers the practical advantages of a wider-ranging pattern of social integration. These new and often overlapping cultural constructions, "tribesman" and "citizen," provide coherence and dynamism, continuity and contemporaneity in modern Jordan.

The King has been accused of being retrogressive and of trying to hold back the country from achieving political maturity because of his repeated defense of Jordan's tribal heritage.[48]

We are Arabs and we shall not neglect our worthy customs and lose our distinctive char-

acteristics inherited from our noble ancestors...The traditional customs, of which we
are justly proud, will continue to be observed.[49]

I believe that in this regard his critics are
misguided. The continuing force of tribal identity does not preclude full participation in the
civil life of the nation.[50] The most serious internal challenge is not the integration of Jordan's Bedouin tribes, but rather, the integration
of Jordan's Palestinian majority.[51] Whether one
prefers the term "subjugated," "encapsulated," or
"integrated," the tribal elements of Jordanian society have become full participants and are, on
the whole, strongly committed to the continuity
and welfare of the State. We have noted the mer-
its of culturally-rooted national identity. However, tribal heritage is a cultural resource and,
as such, may be used in many ways. If "tribalism"
were to be used as an ethnic definition of national identity ("The true Jordanian is a tribal Jordanian"), thereby excluding most of the Palestinian population, then "tribalism" could indeed be a
threat to the State.[52]

TABLE 5.1

Election Results: Selected Subdistricts, Balqa Governorate

MUSLIM CANDIDATES	D.A.	Shuna	Fuhais	Baq'ah	Total
Marwan Abdl Halim al-Nimr al-Hamoud	481	336	790	1402	10762
Zohair al-Zoqan al-Hussein	378	110	917	219	7664
Jamal Abdl Karim Abu Buqar	1289	709	406	528	6861
'Aakaf Fahad al-'Adwan	12	3273	999	882	6470
Saoud M. al-Khrabshah	44	226	210	2067	6268
M. Amin Ziyad al-Kilani	116	138	32	1976	5228
Abdl Karim Hamad al-Faour	4445	8	39	203	4885
Fahad Abdl Halim al-Arab	156	118	4?	754	4656
M. Abdl Razaq Mustafa al-Daoud	296	109	130	605	4181
'Aqab Ahmad Hassan Abu Raman	148	58	270	353	2887
Faiz Zeidan Hamdan Masalhah	1866	51	58	255	2827
M. Raja al-Mous'od Kharisat	148	57	0	434	2495
Kamal Darwad M. al-'Abdalat	184	60	5	167	2237
Hamdan Salim M. al-Z'abi al-'Awamarah	2	4	7	1	786
Khalid Mousa al-Salah al-'Awadat	7	3	39	8	750
Ibrahim Fahad Nimir al-'Awamalah	16	22	26	7	621
Hussein Ahmad Ali Abu Raman	9	2	3	42	600
Kadhim Muhammad Dib 'Awad	0	14	2	151	180
District Totals	9597	5312	3978	10054	171934

138

TABLE 5.1 cont.

CHRISTIAN CANDIDATES	D.A.	Shuna	Fuhais	Baq'ah	Total
Fawzi Shaker T'aimah Daoud	981	2359	1294	281	7694
Raja'i Salah al-Mu'ashir	1298	148	?44	427	7312
Jamal Abdoh al-Sha'ar	596	127	?	21?	6520
Salam Jarish al-Nahas	140	234	214	1686	3070
Farid Salim 'Akroush	158	23	423	62	1483
Ghalab Salah Abu Jabr	117	166	19	249	1276
Bashir Suliman Dibabnah	48	26	23	39	1074
Hanna Ibrahim Hatr	7	5	695	69	501
Jaodat Abduallah al-Akroush	17	46	5	113	292
District Totals	3362	3134	3222	3141	29222

Results published in *al-Dustour* 3-22-1984.
Key:
D.A. = Deir Alla Subdistrict, Shuna = South Shuna Subdistrict,
Total = governorate total, M. = Muhammad.

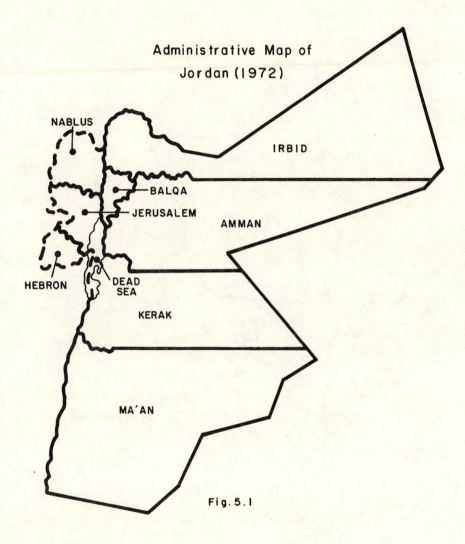

Administrative Map of
Jordan (1972)

NABLUS

IRBID

BALQA

JERUSALEM

AMMAN

HEBRON

DEAD
SEA

KERAK

MA'AN

Fig. 5.1

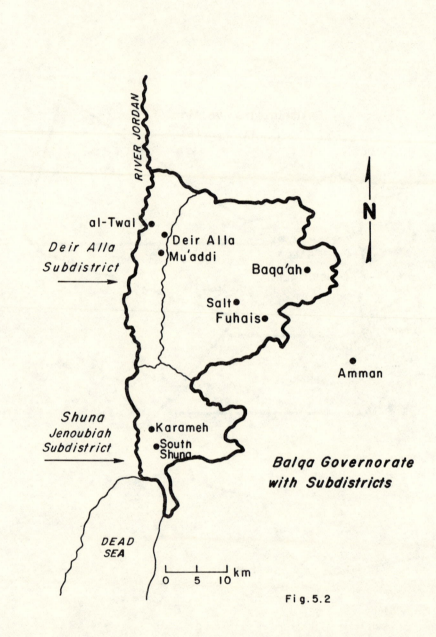

Fig. 5.2

Notes

Acknowledgements. The field research on which this is based was generously supported by a Fulbright-Hays Doctoral Dissertation Research Grant and by a Wenner-Gren Foundation for Anthropological Research Grant-in-Aid. Thanks are due to Dr. A. Sharkas and Governor Khatib for providing me with the election results and for their observations on the election. I am also grateful to Dr. Sharkas for a survey and translation of Arabic-language newspaper articles on the subject. I profited from discussions with Mary Taylor Huber, Linda Jacobs, Rena Lederman, Lawrence Rosen, and Bernard Wilson.

[1] My discussion of "tribalism" and the alternative model of political representation which I am calling meritocratic individualism, relies heavily on the Jordanian press. The section on party politics is drawn from informal meetings with members of Jordan's national elite, from field work in the Jordan Valley, and to a lesser extent on the Jordanian press.

[2] It was this debate concerning the pros and cons of "tribalism" which precipitated the resignation of Minister of Information Leila Sharaf in January 1984.

[3] The new constitution alloted 150 of the 245 seats to Turks and sixty to Arabs despite the fact that the Arab population outnumbered Turks three to one (El-Edroos 1980:8).

[4] Almost immediately after the establishment of the Amirate in 1923 Amir Abdullah set up a committee to formulate a law for the election of a house of parliament. The law was completed in June 1924 and preparations undertaken for elections. But according to Abu Jaber (1969), the British feared a truly popular government and successfully blocked it.

[5] The two minorities were over-represented under the 1928 law with a ratio of one seat for every 5,000 inhabitants for Circassians while allowing the Muslim Arab community only one seat for every 27,000 inhabitants (Aruri in Abu Jaber 1967:40).

[6] According to Harris the Christians were over-represented since they accounted for less than 10 percent (probably about 8 percent) of the population (Harris 1958:84). The Bedouin were ap-

142

pointed by a committee of ten Bedouin leaders.
[7] In 1958 the Lower House was enlarged to fifty seats with two seats reserved for Circassians; seven for Christians; and two for Bedouin. It was increased to the current size of sixty in 1961. In January 1986 the government submitted to Parliament a draft of a new electoral law to replace the electoral law of 1960. The Lower House made a number of amendments to the draft law, endorsed it in March 1986, and passed it on to the Upper House which endorsed the law on April 28, 1986 with no further amendments. The new law increases the number of deputies from sixty to 142 with seventy-one representatives from the West Bank including one seat for Palestinian representatives from each of the eleven refugee camps in Jordan. Six seats are reserved for Bedouin from the eastern desert (*badia*) region--two from the northern, central, and southern badia; nineteen for Christians; and three for Circassians or Chechan.
[8] According to the 1952 constitution, a majority of two-thirds was needed in order for the parliament to withhold confidence in the government (Abu Jaber 1969:231). Today the Lower House has the right to withhold confidence in the government with an absolute majority vote, i.e. at least thirty-one of the total number of sixty members according to article 53 of the constitution. A vote of confidence must be by voice by a roll call of members. (art. 47, cl. I *Internal Rules* of the Parliament); otherwise the vote is usually secret (art. 47, cl. II) (Abu Jaber 1969:245). The Jordanian parliament has only once withheld its confidence in a government, that was in 1963 in the government of Mr. Samir al-Rifai.
[9] The proposed electoral law reasserts Jordan's responsibility for Palestinians in the Israeli-occupied West Bank and in Jordan.
[10] The six vacant seats representing the West Bank were filled by means of an internal election within the parliament since elections could not be held on the West Bank due to Israeli occupation.
[11] Although Article 6:22 and 23 of the constitution provides for women's political, economic and social equality, Jordan's Electoral and Municipal Laws denied women the right to vote. The Electoral Law was amended in April 1974 and the

Municipal Law in April 1982 making women eligible to vote and run for office in national and municipal elections (*The Jordan Times* 3-19-1984).

[12] The minimum voting age is twenty. Citizens could register in any governorate, regardless of their residence. This allowed for some manipulation. For instance, some of the candidates purportedly bused supporters into the governorate where they were running to register and again on election day.

[13] Thirty-six ran for the single vacant position in Amman; eighteen ran for the two Muslim vacancies in Balqa and nine candidates for the single Christian opening there; sixteen for the single vacant seat in Irbid; eighteen for the two vacant seats in Karak; three for the Tafileh seat.

[14] See Layne (1986b) for a comparison. I do not suggest that African "tribalism" is comparable to Middle Eastern "tribalism." In fact, I question whether there is such a thing as African or Middle Eastern "tribalism."

[15] However, no one considered that the settlers or colonialists required direct study themselves.

[16] Here, suffice it to note several of the things such an approach overlooks. This focus on ethnic aspects of populations has concealed other societal divisions such as class differentiations, generational tensions, rural-urban differences. Furthermore, a lack of positive identification with the nation-state is more likely to be the result of perception people have about the regime than because of a sense of ethnic group attachment and loyalty.

[17] Geertz defines a "primordial tie" as "one that stems from the "givens"...of social existence" and contrasts such ties with loyalties to class, party, profession (Geertz 1973:261).

[18] In this way the Jordanian definition of "tribalism" is not unlike that endorsed by western cultural ecologists and modernization theorists who see tribal societies as an evolutionary stage. For instance, in Sahlins' book *Tribesmen* (1968) tribal culture is described as the form of social organization which displaced Paleolithic hunting and gathering societies and which was inturn displaced by "civilizations."

See Clifford (1986) for an analysis of a similar case concerning the authenticity of an American Indian tribe in which many aspects of Mashpee lives such as being a businessman, traveling to Hawaii, or being Baptist, contradicted with the dominant culture's idea of what it means to be an American Indian.

[19] This holds true equally for those who are "for" tribalism. (See for instance Keilani's article in *The Jordan Times* 2-13-1985).

[20] Political scientists have found that family ties play a more important role in American electoral behavior than has been previously understood. Rather than listening to the appeals of candidates with an open mind and reaching a choice based on the issues, American citizens have what is essentially a "standing decision," a long-lasting party attachment to which they adhere with only occasional lapses over a number of elections and these attachments are first developed in the childhood home (Stokes 1985).

[21] For example, honor is accrued through acts of courage and generosity among the Bedouin and the ascribed status of birth varies over time as the relative status of different tribes and of particular families within tribes changes.

[22] See Landau (1980) for a comparison of parliamentary elites in Israel, Lebanon and Turkey.

[23] This contradicts an assumption held by modernization theorists that party politics is a stage of political development and that political development is linear.

[24] The Brotherhood was banned in the fall of 1985 during Jordan's rapproachment with Syria.

[25] See Nuseibi (1983) for a discussion of two generations of Arab nationalists in Jordan.

[26] Because of the recent trend toward Islamic fundamentalism throughout the Middle East, these "Islamic" candidates received a great deal of attention in the Jordanian press.

According to a government official, the reason that "Islamic" candidates were successful in the governorates of Amman and Irbid but did not succeed in winning either of the Muslim seats in Balqa is because tribal organization is stronger in Balqa and since there was more than one seat in Balqa, tribes were able to make alliances with each other thereby further increasing their strength.

[27] It is interesting that Mr. Eshbailat was one of only two deputies who voted against the new electoral law. He objected to the distribution of seats on "sectarian, racial, tribal, and regional considerations instead of pure demographic factors." He also called for exclusion of the West Bank from Parliament because of the continuing Israeli occupation (*The Jordan Times* 3-29-1986).

[28] See Dawisha (1983:65) for a discussion of the consolidation of King Hussein's power in Jordan following the June War of 1967.

[29] All figures on voter registration are from a personal communication from Governor Khatib, Governor of Balqa.

[30] A small community of Palestinians who came as refugees in 1948 live in the town of Deir Alla. They are not significant numerically in terms of the Jordan Valley subdistricts.

[31] A recent estimate puts the East Bank Christian population at 125,000 (Gubser 1983:19).

[32] Although a number of Christians including the candidate Raja'a al-Mu'asher, own large farms in the Jordan Valley they number no more than a handful in all and are therefore insignificant in terms of votes in the Valley subdistricts.

[33] For example, Jamal Abu Bugar won 1,289 votes in Deir Alla, 1,034 in the 'Abbad territory of al-'Arda, 1,492 in the neighboring foothill community 'Arida, 620 from the 'Abbad population in Mahas, and 709 votes from the 'Adwan territory to finish third in the election.

[34] The current voting law (1960) does not stipulate a minimum percentage of the electorate required to vote. Although there was speculation that a minimum might be included in the new electoral law, none was.

[35] Each of the candidates had the right to station a representative in each of the polling places to ensure fairness. Most candidates could not recruit enough representatives for each of the voting stations so at any given station some but not all of the candidates would be likely to be represented. In the Deir Alla Subdistrict local girls served as representatives for local candidates and for some of the Christian candidates from Salt in the women's polling stations.

[36] If men tried to enter female voting stations to "help" their women vote they were pre-

vented from doing so by the voting committee.
[37] Unfortunately, I do not know how the in-
tra-tribal negotiation to select tribal representatives took place. I did visit the Mayor's office
in South Shuna the week before the election and
learned that the negotiations concerning who would
represent the 'Adwan tribe were still hotly underway.
[38] Bedouins have had the least turnover of
any group in providing national representatives
with representation coming from only five families
during the period from 1928-1947. For instance,
Hamd Ibn Jazi, sheikh of sheikhs of the South Jordanian Bedouin tribes was elected to every Legislative Council from 1928-1947 and was elected in
the   first   five   parliamentary   elections
(1950-1956). Upon his death his son Faisal succeeded him (Abu Jaber 1969:237).
[39] Among the 'Abbad and Mashalkhah tribes the
terminology for different tribal groups is used
ambiguously, probably because usage is changing.
Although all agree that a *qabilah* is bigger and
usually more prestigious than an *'ashirah* which in
turn is bigger than a *'ailah* (family), there is no
consensus as to which of these terms should be
used for a particular group. The term *hamulah*
(lineage), was not used by these Bedouin.
[40] For example, after the death in 1981 of
Ahmad al-Naim, the sheikh of the Mashalkhah,
Sheikh Ahmad's eldest son, Salah, replaced him as
head of the al-Naim family but the other Mashalkhah tribes do not recognize him as a paramount
sheikh. Each tribe is now led by its own sheikh.
Another example of the fragmentation of large tribal groupings is the matter of blood vengeance.
Although tribes still act corporately in matters
of blood vengeance, they do so at a lower structural level. The range of responsibility for
crimes has gradually been reduced by the State.
(See Oweidi 1982:27 for details).
[41] It is doubtful, even if the alliances had
not been abrogated whether the tribesmen and women
of the Deir Alla Subdistrict would have voted for
him at their sheikh's bidding. In addition to
3,273 votes from his home subdistrict, South Shuna, 'Aakaf al-'Adwan profited from an alliance
with the victorious Christian candidate Dr. Fawzi
Daoud and as a result won nearly one thousand

votes in the Christian town of Fuhais (the largest
number of votes for a Muslim candidate there).
They were one of the few coalitions which appeared
together in newspaper advertisements.

The second place winner, Zouhair al-Zoqan,
also received strong support from Fuhais, winning
918 votes there. Apparently, the Christians of
Fuhais, unlike the Jordan Valley Bedouin, were
willing to vote as a group for candidates from
tribes with whom their group had made alliances.

[42] Furthermore, the segmentary proclivities
of the tribe may be extended to broader levels.
Hence, the segmentary model may serve to identify
local with national interests; each level being
used as a metaphor for another. See Herzfeld
(1985) and Layne (1986a) for a fuller discussion
of this process.

[43] One of the babies he delivered, now a
highschool senior, worked as his representative in
Mu'addi.

[44] In addition to being an occasion on which
individuals asserted their identity as citizens by
exercizing their right to vote, the elections were
also used as a celebration of tribal identity.
The women who worked as representatives for candidates in the voting stations in the Jordan Valley
wore traditional embroidered tribal dresses instead of their normal everyday western wear.

[45] Members of the Jordan Valley Bedouin
tribes have supported Arab political parties in
other contexts and will probably do so again in
the future. Many middle-aged Bedouin men told me
that they had supported Nassir in the 1950s, and
several of the banned political parties have a
following among young, educated tribesmen and women in the Jordan Valley today. Many members of
the Almuni Club of the Middle Ghor in the Jordan
Valley consider themselves to be supporters of the
Iraqi Ba'th Party, the Syrian Ba'th, or the Communist Party, in that order of popular support. The
annual club elections were dominated by these parties in 1982 and 1983. Yet during the 1984 parliamentary elections, these same individuals did
not organize or participate according to party
lines.

[46] Following the election, there was a reaction to the onslaught against "tribalism" and the
King and others published letters in the local pa-

pers supporting tribes. Obviously the distinction between "tribalism" and "tribes" was not adequately clear, and some feared that the attack of "tribalism" would alienate Jordan's tribal population. See Layne (1986a) for a fuller discussion of the new meanings of Bedouin identity in Jordan today.

[47] The government has followed a number of policies designed to encourage the development of the feeling of national unity among the Bedouin. For instance, the 1973 amendments to the Bedouin Control Laws did away with the Bedouin distinction between cousin's compensation for crimes (*diyah*) and foreigner's compensation in accordance with the official position that all Jordanians are cousins and brothers, "a group of one family" (*usrah wahidah*) (Oweidi 1982:41). The decreasing authority of tribal sheikhs can be seen as another manifestation of this process.

[48] This disdain for Jordan's cultural heritage on the part of some of its intellectuals is in strong contrast with the pressing concern in many parts of North Africa for cultural authenticity and the rejection of any apparent influence from European colonization. This difference may be a result of the relatively small British presence and short colonial period in Jordan.

[49] Excerpt from Hussein's address to the Badiyah Police Headquarters in 1976 quoted in Oweidi (1982). For another example see his letter to the Prime Minister January 28, 1985.

[50] Nor is the opposite position taken recently by Jureidini and McLaurin (1984) correct--that Jordan risks instability because the strength of tribal consciousness is waning.

[51] The King is well aware of this challenge. In a letter to Mr. Obeidat, Prime Minister of the new government instituted in January, 1984 shortly before the elections, the King expressed the hope that "Democratic life should serve to extend and deepen the national unity of this country and should display a strong cohesion between the peoples of the two banks of the Jordan river...who share a common destiny" (*The Jordan Times* 1-11-1984).

[52] See for example the demonstration by Bedouin tribes in October 1979 calling for "Jordan for Jordanians" (*al-Urdun 'l l-Urduniyin*) described in Oweidi (1982).

149

Appendix A

Chronology of Major Events
in Jordan's Legislative History

1921 Amir Abdullah arrives in Jordan

1923 Transjordanian Amirate established by Britain
     British Resident appointed in Amman

1928 Organic Law of Jordan promulgated

1946 Hashemite Kingdom of Jordan established
     Constitution promulgated

1947 First Parliament (twenty elected members)

1950 Union of East and West Banks
     Second Parliament (forty elected members)

1951 King Abdullah assassinated
     Third Parliament
     New constitution rendering the government
     responsible to Parliament

1953 King Hussein ascends the throne
     Fourth Parliament

1954 Most political parties dissolved

1956 Fifth Parliament, General Glubb dismissed

1958 Lower House enlarged to fifty members

1957 Coup attempt, all parties banned

1961 Sixth Parliament (sixty elected members)

1962 Seventh Parliament

1963 Eighth Parliament

1967 Ninth Parliament, Six-Day War with Israel

1974 Women enfranchised
     Ninth Parliament suspended

150

1978 Consultative Council established (seventy-
     five appointed members)

1984 Parliament reconvened, by-elections held

Appendix B

Campaign flyer for Hani Khair
A Muslim Candidate in the Governorate of Amman

1) I believe in God and the dignity of man and his freedom.
2) I believe in the full unity of the two Banks which was and never ceases to be a shining model of Arab unity.
3) I believe in Jordan as a steadfast Arab nation and as a bridge between Arab society and the world.
4) I believe that the energy of the citizens should be released to express itself in agriculture and industry. "Citizens should eat what they plant and wear what they make." (Khalil Gibran)
5) I believe that we should take pride in citizens as soldiers, civil servants, drivers, teachers, farmers, professionals, poets, writers, artists, sportsmen: each in his own place and field and that we should respect the principle of equal opportunity for work for all without discrimination.
6) I am proud of nuclear families (father, mother, children) as the basis of extended families and I support the role of women in making life dignified and their ability to give and their mission in making a balanced society and the participation of women with men in pushing the nation forward.
7) I believe that certain laws which are not suited to the needs and rights of Jordanian citizens should be modified, specifically the laws concerning public elections, education, retirement, the press, traffic, and military service recruitment.
8) I will work to enhance public freedom for people's decision making.
I love Jerusalem as I love Amman. God is the guidance.

(Translated by Dr. A. Sharkas.)

Chapter VI

TRIBAL DEMOCRACY:

THE ANATOMY OF PARLIAMENTARY ELECTIONS IN
KUWAIT

Nicolas Gavrielides

Introduction

Founded in the beginning of the 18th century,
Kuwait continued to be a city-state until the discovery and exploitation of oil after the Second
World War.[1] Tribally organized, the city has been
ruled by the Sabah Lineage of the powerful Aniza
tribe since the eighteenth century. In the past,
the rulers were able to provide security by carefully using their desert tribal ties and by re-
cruiting tribesmen as warriors, retainers, merchants, and pearl divers. Being of noble tribal
descent, a warrior, or a merchant placed a person
at the height of the social hierarchy. Social patronage based on tribal principles provided the
bases for a complex hierarchy of social relations
between the urbanized tribesmen and their desert
brethren as well as between the tribal Arabs, the
non-tribal Arabs and the few non-Arabs who lived
in the city. An ethnic division of labor was the
prevailing mode with caravan trade, seafaring,
pearl diving, and herding being the chief occupations.
Despite the dramatic politico-economic changes which followed the discovery oil in Kuwait, the
tribally-organized social structure continues to
prevail. Tribal ideology provided the rationale

and symbols with which the large influx of foreign
labor, both Arab and non-Arab, were incorporated.
In addition the tribal ideology provided for the
settlement of a large number of desert tribesmen
in Kuwait who came as clients of the Sabah. These
tribesmen became an important electoral constituency. It is with this tribal settlement in mind
that the Kuwaiti elections are analyzed. I argue
that in a state such as Kuwait where tribal ideology is in operation, tribal demographics and tribal social structure are essential elements in the
modern political game of free parliamentary
elections.

History of Kuwait's Representational Government

In 1961 the United Kingdom and Kuwait terminated the 1899 agreement which had given the UK
responsibility for the conduct of Kuwait's foreign
policy. Kuwait became a fully independent state
on June 19, 1961. The ruling Sheikh, Sheikh Abdallah al-Salim took the new title of Amir, and
Kuwait was admitted as a member of the Arab
League. In December 1961 an election was held to
choose twenty members of the Constituent Assembly
(the other members being ministers). This Assembly drafted a new constitution under which a National Assembly of fifty members was elected in
January 1963 and Sheikh Sabah al-Salim al-Sabah,
the heir apparent,[2] was Prime Minister of the new
council of ministers. In January 1965 a constitutional crisis reflecting the tension between the
paternalist ruling house and the democratically-
minded National Assembly resulted in the formation
of a strengthened Cabinet. In November 1965
Sheikh Abdallah died and was succeeded by Sheikh
Sabah. His post as prime minister was taken over
by the new heir apparent, Crown Prince Sheikh Jaber al-Ahmad.

In response to public opinion, the ruling
family permitted the Assembly election of January
1971 to be held on the basis of a free vote,
though women, illiterates and non-Kuwaitis still
have no voting rights. There was a lively
election campaign with 184 candidates (thirty
years of age or over) contesting the fifty seats.

Despite the non-existence of political parties
which are still illegal, several members and supporters of the Arab Nationalist Movement, founded
in the 1950s by Dr. George Habash were elected.
This radical group led by Dr. Ahmad al-Khatib was
generally regarded as the principal opposition to
the government. After the 1971 elections the
Crown Prince was reappointed Prime Minister and
formed a new Cabinet. The representation of the
ruling family was reduced from five to three, and
for the first time, the Cabinet included two ministers drawn from the elected members of the National Assembly.

After the election in 1975 a sixteen-member
Cabinet was appointed with the Crown Prince continuing as Prime Minister. In August 1976 the
Amir suspended the National Assembly on the
grounds that, among other things, it had been de-
laying legislation. A committee was ordered to be
formed to review the Constitution. On December
31, 1977 the Amir Sheikh Sabah died and was succeeded by his cousin the Crown Prince, Sheikh Jabir al-Ahmad al-Sabah. The new Crown Prince was
Sheikh Sa'ad al-Abdallah al-Salim al-Sabah. A
fifty-member committee was set up in early 1980 to
consider constitutional amendments and a revised
form of legislature. Following its recommendations, a royal decree provided for the election of
a new assembly before the end of February 1981.
Despite the uncertainty generated by the Gulf War,
the election campaign went ahead, with as many as
448 candidates contesting the fifty seats. The
franchise was limited to the 90,000 male Kuwaiti
citizens over the age of twenty-one. Of these
less than half (or about 3% of the population)
registered to vote. The fifth National Assembly
was elected on February 23, 1981. Fifty assembly
members (two from each of the twenty-five districts) were elected for four-year terms. The
Crown Prince formed a new fifteen-member Cabinet
which included only one elected member of the new
Assembly.

Sociocultural Background

The political and economic prominence of the small city-state of Kuwait prior to the discovery of oil in the 1930s was based on the sociocultural principles upon which the city was organized. These principles which were tribal, provided and continue to provide the ruling family with the strength needed to maintain their rule.[3]

This social structure was based on a desert tribal model which places patrilineal descent groups in a social hierarchy according to an ideology of noble descent. Among *asiil* (pure-noble) tribes, nobility is expressed through blood purity maintained by endogamous marriage rules, camel-breeding, and disdain for manual labor. These noble tribes see themselves also as warriors. Noble camel-breeding tribes are dominant over and protect subservient shepherd tribes and craftsmen-pariah groups. Slaves, although occupying the lowest level in the hierarchy, are able to marry their women into the noble tribes (their masters) and are also able to carry their masters' tribal name (*intisab*).

Society in the state of Kuwait was divided into two main groups, Arabs and non-Arabs. The Arabs in turn were divided into two parallel groups: *arab daar* and *arab hadaar*. The *arab daar* were tribesmen (*badu*) living in the city and its environs serving the Sabahs, and being under their protection. These *arab daar*, some of whom came to the city seasonally, especially during the pearling season, maintained their tribal identity and social relations with their brethren in the desert and acted as liaisons and hosts for their kinsmen in their dealing with the city. The most important of the *arab daar* were the armed retainers serving the rulers of Kuwait and forming its main fighting force. These armed men (*fedawiya*) were recruited from various noble tribes by the Sabahs, by means of their ties of descent and affinity with the noble tribes of the desert. It should be remembered that the Sabahs themselves are members of the noble tribe of Aniza. The *arab daar* also consisted of non-*asiil* tribal groups, who in the city are called *baysari*, meaning impure or hybrid. These *baysari* groups were the shepherds and craftsmen of the desert who performed their services in the city and its surroundings. Slaves were also members of the *arab daar*.

The second group in the city, the *hadaar*, (permanent city dwellers) were also divided into *asiil* and *baysari*. The *asiil* were led by the Sabah ruling family who had political power only, for the Sabahs prior to the exploration of oil did not engage in trade. They were merely a military-political group depending on gifts from the merchants whom they protected in the city. Members of noble tribes living in the city were, for the most part, merchants, sea captains, and pearl divers. The *baysaris* came from lesser tribes or from Arabs with no acknowledged tribal descent and were engaged as divers, seamen, and fishermen. The *asiil* groups in the city, especially the Sabahs and prominent merchants maintained slaves as armed retainers and servants. The slaves of al-Sabah were used to counterbalance the *fedawiya*.

The non-Arab (*ajam*) in the city included a large number of Persians, Baluchis, Indians, Pathans, Kanadira, Awadiyah, and small numbers of Armenians, Greeks, and Jews. Some members of these groups were prominent merchants and sea captains. However, the most menial occupations in the city were also performed by members of such groups.

All people in the city and its environs owed their allegiance to the Sabahs as their protectors and sponsors. This relationship is expressed by the term *mu'azib*, which means host and entails a patron-client relationship according to the tribal model.

After the oil revenues began to have a major impact on the State, the Sabahs consciously strived to maintain the tribal structure with its desert social ideology. Such a structure persists today under a modern veneer. This modern veneer is often deceiving to westerners and western-oriented social scientists and intellectuals. For example, some see in it discrimination and segregation (Hill 1972) while others see a western-style social welfare state (Hijazi 1964).

With oil revenues, the Sabahs acquired a powerful economic base in addition to their traditional political-military role. The acquisition

of economic control occurred gradually through
their use of legal acumen. By law every Sabah
adult receives a monthly stipend from the treas-
ury. The bulk of the Sabah wealth has its origin
in real estate. Members of the Sabah family owned
real estate in their quarter in the old city.
When the old city began to be demolished to make
room for modern roads and to become a modern commercial and administrative center, the owners of
real estate in the city were rewarded handsomely
for their loses through a process called *tathmin*,
meaning appraisal. Since the center city was the
first to be demolished, people who owned real estate there had "a head start". In addition, a
person's social rank reflected the price of compensation. The people whose land was expropriated
were also given choice plots to build new houses
in carefully designed suburbs. In addition, members of the Sabah family laid claim to large
tracts of land in the desert outside the city
walls. These lands became the modern suburbs.
Their owners were also compensated by the government. They sold parts of this land to other Kuwaitis in areas designated for the habitation of
non-Kuwaitis. Apartment buildings were built on
such lands and rented either to the government to
house non-Kuwaiti government employees or outright
to non-Kuwaitis.

With the capital acquired from the sale of
land to the government, the Sabahs either became
merchants in their own right or silent partners
with non-Kuwaitis, especially Palestinians and
Iranians. Some of the largest and most modern
apartment buildings in Kuwait today are owned by
Shaykhs and Shaykhas (female shaykhs). In addition to acquiring capital through real estate, the
Sabahs also used their political positions in the
operation of the government social services programs to acquire wealth.

Prominent members of the Sabah family (it is
reported that there are four degrees of Sabahs as
there are two degrees of Kuwaiti citizenship) who
could not for political reasons, in keeping with
the formalities of the old tribal model, engage
openly in trade forced certain prominent *ajam*
merchants to enter into silent partnerships with
them. In addition to engaging in business ven-

tures in Kuwait, as they began to accumulate substantial amounts of capital, the Sabahs began investing overseas.

The old tribal merchant families in Kuwait resent the Sabah's acquisition of wealth and economic power on top of their traditional political power. In providing basic social services to the population free of charge through the government, the Sabah family see themselves as fulfilling their ultimate ideal role of *mu'azibs*. Perhaps this is why prominent tribal merchant families refuse such services today in an act of defiance and instead seek such services in private schools, hospitals, etc. where the costs are very high. These urbanites also feel outnumbered and out-maneuvered by the naturalization of tribesmen. This is a source of resentment because the Bedouin and their dependents are in their view non-productive--refusing to perform any productive labor but demanding services which necessitate the importation of foreigners (al-Nafisi 1978:29, Farah 1980:34). As will be seen in our discussion of the 1985 election, the tribesmen and the old urban merchants have been pitted against each other politically. They also believe that the Sabahs manipulated the Kuwaiti stock market for the benefit of new bedouin merchants. The role these urban merchants played in parliament will be discussed later.

The Sabahs expect loyalty from their clients who enjoy the services of the welfare state. Such services are provided to citizens only. Non-citizens have partial access to services depending on their *mu'azib*. Over half the population of Kuwait is classified as non-Kuwaiti and this classification legally prohibits them from owning a business or land. Hence, the non-Kuwaitis are not only workers, but also the consumers who keep the Kuwaitis in business.

Tribesmen have the best chance of acquiring citizenship. Informants report that the ultimate test for eligibility is an interview by the citizenship committee to determine the authenticity of a person's claim to tribal affiliation. After the advent of the oil era, the Sabahs began granting citizenship to large numbers of select tribal groups. Such tribesmen are engaged as soldiers,

police, guards, and special retainers--a modern
form of the *fedawiya*. When tribesmen first arrived
in Kuwait, they simply camped at the outskirts of
the city as they always had in the past. Gradually the camp developed into a shanty town (*'ashiish*).
As select members of such tribal groups have been
granted citizenship, they have been given houses
which are constructed in designated suburbs for
tribesmen only. The residential patterns in Kuwait are shown on Figures 6.1.

In addition to housing, new citizens are provided with free access to services such as education, health care, and a job which sometimes ex-
ists only on paper. Some tribesmen are reported
to be triple citizens of Kuwait, Saudi Arabia, and
Bahrain, reaping benefits from all three "welfare
states". If a job is materially present, it is a
non-manual one in keeping with the ideal tribal
disdain for manual labor (*hurfa*). The uneducated
prefer government jobs in the army and the police.
The educated who work in the government bureaucracy have preference over non-Kuwaitis for promotion
to managerial positions. If a tribesman has to
work for himself at a second job, he drives a
taxi. Driving a taxi is not considered manual labor. Non-Kuwaitis are not allowed to own taxis.
The children of these tribesmen are encouraged and
even pushed to acquire at least a high school education and often advanced degrees. They pursue
this aggressively, for they realize education is
their only avenue to positions with access to power in the government other than military service.
Members of the Sabah family encourage this by providing special scholarships for children of
tribesmen to pursue graduate and professional
studies abroad. When they graduate, such tribesmen are placed in strategic government and private
sector positions to counterbalance the other established groups such as the *hadaar* and *ajam*.

Specific tribal groups are patronized by certain members of the Sabah family. A very powerful
tribal group in Kuwait today is the Ajman tribe
whose members are also the *akhwal* (mothers' brothers) of a segment of the Sabah family. The present Amir of Kuwait was reported to have married
over one hundred and thirty times as of the summer
of 1979. All such marriages have been with noble

tribal women. He maintains only four wives at one time in accordance with Islamic law. I was also told that lately the Sabahs have been refusing to give their daughters in marriage to noble tribes as they did in the past, thus setting themselves apart as a very special social group. This is resented by other prominent tribal groups who see this as an attempt by the Sabahs to establish a royal dynasty contrary to the egalitarian principles governing *asiil* tribal groups.

Non-tribal Arabs, especially Palestinians, and non-Arab groups such as Indians, Pakistanis, Baluchis and Pathans are permitted to live and work in Kuwait under the patronage of the Sabahs. All such groups are expected to show loyalty to the Sabahs through a vast and complicated patronage network which is basically economic and reciprocal. These groups are kept under control by counterbalancing each other through the "division of labor by ethnic group" described by Carlton Coon (1953). For example, Christians from Goa in India work exclusively as maids and governesses for urban Kuwaiti families. I have heard people refer to "our Indian female" (*hindiyitna*) meaning "our female Indian *maid*" (italics mine). Baluchis are employed as door keepers by Kuwaiti families, while Egyptians from lower Egypt are employed as door keepers in apartment buildings owned by Kuwaitis but inhabited by non-Kuwaitis. Nubians are employed as cooks. Egyptian teachers teach religion, social sciences and humanities, while Palestinian teachers teach English and science. Syrians from Houran operate tire repair stores; Armenians from Aleppo who were previously brass workers now operate car body repair shops. Sykhs from India maintain car spare parts stores. Pakistanis work as bank clerks while those educated Palestinians who are not teachers work in insurance. Arabs from Iran are laborers, Yemenis from Mahra operate clothing stores, and Lebanese operate ultra-modern department stores. Omanis are messengers and poor Egyptians are garbage collectors.

As mentioned earlier, the tribal Arabs despise manual labor which signifies subservience and subordination. Oil wealth has enabled Kuwaitis to have manual and menial labor occupations performed by non-Kuwaitis. Non-*asiil* and pariah groups such as the *Sulluba* and *Suna'* who performed such tasks in the past are not engaged in them today. In a sense, such groups have been pushed up in the almost caste-like hierarchy, being replaced by non-tribal Arabs and non-Arabs. Today such pariah groups are being rewarded for their loyalty by the Sabahs by providing them with the opportunity not to perform tasks which are considered menial in the tribal ideology. So, economically at least, these groups feel as if they are not outcasts anymore.

However, socially, they remain *baysari* and no *asiil* tribe will intermarry with them. Non-*asiil* groups are trying different techniques in order to overcome their socially subservient position within the tribal system of hierarchy. For example, some groups who were shepherds like the Awazim and other groups who were smiths such as the Rashaydah have attempted to prove their "noble" descent by publishing genealogies which link them to noble tribal ancestors. Noble tribes, on the other hand, never publish their genealogies. To crystalize such an important part of the oral tradition would deprive it of one of its most important features, its flexibility, which responds to popular opinion and changing circumstances.

The *Suna'* and *Sulluba*, who cannot or will not dabble in the art of manipulating genealogies, have attained legislation which forbids the use of the term *Sullubi* or its equivalent as a term of address or reference. I had to obtain special permission as a professor using a *mu'azib* in order to consult books which use these terms (e.g. Dickson 1956 and Azawi 1936). The director of the municipal library in Kuwait had such books under lock and key. Other non-*asiil* tribesmen have successfully integrated themselves into noble tribes such as the Dafiir, which in fact is seen as a confederation (*tahaluf*) in return for loyalty. On the other hand, I have known tribesmen who had been rejected by the tribe of Utaybah when they invoked the principle of *intisab* on the grounds that they were the *Suna'* of Utaybah. Ex-slaves, however, are still socially and economically attached to their tribes and masters and carry tribal names.

Figures 6.1, 6.2 and 6.3 show the distribution of urban Arab Kuwaitis, tribal Kuwaitis, non-
Kuwaiti tribesmen living in *'ashiish*, and other non-
Kuwaitis. This distribution shows the spatial
segregation in Kuwait. The significance of social
segregation for political behavior, especially in
parliamentary elections will be discussed below.

Tribal Politics and Political Groups From 1960-1976

The spatial distribution of tribal and ethnic groups in Kuwait became especially significant
during the sixties and seventies when residential
tribal districts were made into voting districts.
During that period the *arab hadaar*, the tribal
group, and the Islamic groups were the most important political groups.

The *hadaar* were, in the 1960s and 1970s,
mainly liberal reformists who challenged the Sabahs and resented their newly acquired economic
strength. This group was represented by a club
called Nadi al-Istiqlal.

By bringing in a large number of tribesmen
from the desert, and by granting them citizenship
and concentrating them in specific locales, the
Sabahs have been able to have loyal supporters under arms and in parliament. The tribesmen formed
a solid block and voted in support for their *mu'a-
zibs*.

In the 1960s and 1970s Islamic Fundamentalism, represented by Jam'iyat al-Islah, was a force
to be reckoned with in Kuwait.[4] Kuwait's Sunni
Fundamentalists are a branch of the Saudi Wahhabi
Ikhwan and are acknowledged as *salafiyyin* (fundamentalists) by the Wahhabi *Ikhwan's* leader, Juhayman
Ibn Sayf al-Utaybi (Utaybi n.d.:7).[5] The leader of
Jam'iyat al-Islah, Shaykh al-Rifa'i is Sunni, but
his repeated election to parliament from a Shia
district prior to 1981 signifies the alliance
which operated up until the Iranian Revolution in
1978 between the Shia and the Sunni Fundamentalists in Kuwait.

The fundamentalists in Kuwait have been tolerated and appeased by the Kuwaiti authorities at
times and persecuted at others. For example, during the operation of the parliament in the sixties

and seventies the Sunni fundamentalists were allied with the Shia and the tribal block. They sponsored legislation which provided for the building of mosques, the application of Islamic law in civil matters, and the teaching of religion in schools. The Shia and tribal members voted in support of such legislation. In return for allowing the tribal block to vote for such measures, the Sabahs assured the fundamentalist and Shia votes against liberal legislation sponsored by the liberal urban merchants. The government also allowed Jam'iyat al-Islah to use a bulldozer and raze the shrine of al-Khadr in the Island of Faylaka in 1966, saints' shrines being considered as *bid'a* (innovation) by the Wahhabis (Utaybi n.d.:6).

When the alliance between the fundamentalists, the Shia, and the tribal block began to break in 1976, the Sabahs suspended the parliament. With the advent of the Iranian revolution, the Shia and the fundamentalists demonstrated in Kuwait. The government reacted by closing Jam'-iyat al-Islah and then calling parliament back into session. Parliament was then dissolved and new elections were called. Table 6.4 summarizes the membership in parliament by ethnic groups and specific tribal groups. Those whose affiliation is not listed are *hadaar* Sunnis from Najd. Although they are of *asiil* stock they are not socially considered to be tribesmen. These are Arab urbanites mainly composed of the old merchant families from Najd such as al-Ghanim, al-Saqr, al-Jana'at, al-Sayf, al-Badr, al-Jaliil and al-Salih, and prominent merchant families from southern Iraq.

The *hadaar* members of parliament dropped from twenty-two in 1963 to fourteen in 1975. The Shia membership doubled from six in 1963 to twelve in 1975. During the same period, the tribal block rose from twenty to twenty-two with the increase coming, for the most part, from desert tribes.[6] This was the beginning of an important trend which fully developed in the 1985 election.

The 1981 Elections

For the first four parliamentary elections in Kuwait (between 1963-1975) Kuwait was divided into ten voting districts each of which elected five members of Parliament (Asiri and al-Manufi 1986:98). These districts were made up of the following social groups. In 1981 the above ten districts were reorganized by dividing them into twenty-five districts, each having two deputies instead of five, thus keeping the total of fifty members. This reorganization significantly effected the outcome of the 1981 and 1985 elections. (See Table 6.2 and Appendix B for the details of redistricting and Table 6.3 for members of the 1981 Parliament by affiliation.) The result of this redistricting was that the seats in predominantly tribal districts increased from twenty-five to thirty-one, the seats in predominantly Shia districts decreased from ten to four, and seats in the predominantly *hadaar* districts remained at fifteen.

Because many voting districts have mixed populations as shown on Table 6.1, even though the Liberal/Left had a following in districts with fifteen seats in the 1981 elections, they were not able to elect a single deputy. Their setback was mostly due to the division of old districts (2), (6), and (8) (See Appendix B). Very little time was allowed between redistricting and the 1981 election so that the Liberal/Left was not able to reorganize in order to face the fundamentalist trend of the early 1980s (Asiri and al-Manufi 1986:100). Due to the division of the old districts, a large number of Liberal/Left candidates competed for at least half the previous votes. This resulted in splitting votes and the gain for fundamentalists or independents (*al-Watan* 2-19-1985). None of the eighteen *hadaar* deputies openly identified with the Liberal/Left but a large number were fundamentalists.

The Shia representation fell from ten in 1975 to five in 1981. The Shia suffered a setback simply because of the reduction of deputies from their districts due to redistricting.

The tribal deputies rose from twenty-two in 1975 to twenty-seven in 1981. The tribes gained

over all due to redistricting but the smaller
tribes benefited especially. Because the new districts tended to have a larger number of tribal
candidates sharing a smaller number of votes, the
smaller tribes were able to elect deputies in several instances when the larger tribes split their
votes between districts. Three tribes will serve
as an example. The large Ajman tribe had seven
deputies in the 1975 Parliament. In 1981 they
managed to elect only four. They have a heavy
concentration in new districts (19), (21), (22),
and (23) with a total of eight possible deputies
while in 1975 they were concentrated in districts
(3) and (10) with a possible total of ten deputies. (See Table 6.4 for tribal concentrations
with electoral percentage in the new electoral
districts). In contrast, the smaller Awazim tribe
which had only five deputies in the 1975 Parliament was able to elect eight in 1981. This is due
to the fact that in the new districts (12), (13),
(25) and (24) they are predominant (See Table
6.4). Similarly, the Mutayr doubled its deputies
from two in 1975 to four in 1981. They predomi-
nated in old district (4) while in 1981 they pre-
dominated in new district (17) and partially in
new districts (22), (16) and (15).

Primary Elections

In 1985 Kuwait witnessed a new phenomenon in
its electoral process, namely electoral primaries.
The most compelling reason leading to the institution of primaries was the experience of the 1981
redistricting. The 1981 elections were characterized by a smaller number of voters per district.
This caused the Liberal/Left and specific tribes
to lose many seats because many votes were "wasted" or "scattered". Tribes who had large concentrations saw their winning deputies dwindle. With
smaller districts, a large number of candidates
was detrimental.

In 1985 the Liberal/Left dealt with the problem of smaller districts by reducing the number of
candidates in the districts where they had a
chance to win. This took place in districts (18),
(14), (11), (10), (9), (8), (7), (6), (3), and

(2). They also ran candidates who were tribal in tribal districts such as district (18). As a result, they managed to elect thirteen deputies in 1985, four of whom were tribal. This was quite a comeback following their complete failure in the 1981 election when they were unable to elect a single candidate. Another tactic which the Liberal/Left used (also used by the tribes) was for their supporters to vote only for one candidate the Liberal/Left candidate, and not to use their right for a second vote, thus depriving candidates who opposed them and also depriving "neutral" candidates from gaining a plurality. This tactic called *al-sawt al-awar*, the one-eyed vote was used in districts where the Liberal/Left was strong but not strong enough to field two candidates and insure their success.

The tribes adopted a modern structural tactic in order to eliminate competition among their members in the new smaller districts. This new tactic was primary elections (*intikhabat far'iyah*). These elections occurred only in tribal districts (See Table 6.4) and became, in and of themselves, one of the campaign issues of the 1985 elections. The Liberal/Leftists, fundamentalists, and merchant/*hadaar* opposed primaries on the grounds that they promoted tribalism and sectarianism, characteristics considered inappropriate and detrimental to a modern state. The tribes responded by saying that tribal primary elections insure that the tribe can put forward the best candidate and prevent the possibility of less qualified candidates gaining a plurality in a situation where a large number of candidates compete for a small number of votes. One tribal argument in favor of primaries even went as far as to say that "if Ronald Reagan can have primaries, so can we." A tangible result of the primaries was that the number of candidates in 1985 was 265 while in 1981 it was 534 with most of the drop coming from the tribal districts (*al-Anba'* 1985).

The significance of tribal primaries in Kuwait goes beyond their immediate impact on the outcome of the 1985 elections. The very fact that they occured at all was of importance. Primaries did not occur among the Liberal/Left, the Fundamentalists, the Shia or the urban merchants, but only among tribal groups. Why? The answer to

this question is related to the nature of tribalism as a form of social organization and the use
of the Kuwaiti ruling authorities of tribal ideology as the basis upon which they draw the principles, values and symbols of the Kuwaiti state. As
shown in the introduction of this chapter, Kuwaiti
society is a tribal society in terms of its social
structure and ideology.

In the absence of formal political parties
which are illegal in Kuwait, the Shia, the Sunni
Fundamentalist, the Merchants and Liberal/Left do
not have the organizational structure to provide
for a limited number of candidates through a process that their constituents would agree upon.
Tribes, on the other hand, can provide an organizational structure because they, in and of themselves, are a form of kin-based political organization (Fried 1967, Service 1975). Primaries were
an expression of tribal solidarity (us versus
them) and they allowed the members of these tribes
to delicately refine and define their role within
a modern political arena which has a formal vehi-
cle for popular political participation through
parliamentary elections. In addition to having an
indigenous political structure which allowed them
to reach a consensus, their members endorse egalitarianism and are used to having direct access to
their leaders through the *majlis*, *shura*, and *diwani-
yah*. Modern elections then, do nothing more than
formalize an already existing informal process.

The group membership of tribal organization
(based on descent) offers an already socially accepted entity which can produce a single candidate. The other political forces in Kuwait are
not organized and cannot organize legally. For
the Liberal/Left to hold primaries is to tacitly
declare itself a political party. When a tribe
holds a primary, it does so as a social group, al-
beit a political one, but not according to the way
a modern state defines the term political. Primaries are a political act in as much as they enable
groups to obtain power. Tribal primaries do this
through the use of the organizational principle of
descent and not on the basis of people organizing
around a principle or a point of view (*al-Qabas*
12-27, 28-1984).

Tribes could not act as single units during the primaries. The government redistricting plan made sure that no single tribe is concentrated in one district. Table 6.4 shows the distribution of tribes in fifteen out of the twenty-five electoral districts.

All the tribes did well with redistricting. The primaries enabled them to streamline their candidates. Three tribes gained deputies--Aniza, Rashaydah and Utaybah--all of whom skillfully dealt with the primaries.

Primaries really work to the tribe's advantage when the tribe has about 20% of the vote and it provides one candidate for whom tribal members vote alone without casting their other vote. When a tribe has an absolute majority of the vote, people do not abide by the results of the primaries, yet though a large number of candidates run from the tribe, tribal members still win two seats. For example, in district (15) they conducted a primary which did not hold. Instead of the two winners of the primary running, nine candidates ran from the tribe in this district which had a total of nineteen candidates competing for two seats. Despite all this, two Rashaydah candidates won, one of whom was a winner in the primary. The majority of their candidates had a very small number of votes ranging from three to eighty-five votes. The winners carried 782 and 753 votes (*al-Tali'a* 3-3-1985). The Mutayr have 64.8% of the vote in new district (17). They had a primary but could not agree on two candidates, instead four ran. Nevertheless, their two candidates won.

The Mutayr allied with the Rashaydah in districts (15) and (16) where the Mutayr had only 19.3% and 14.5% of the vote in exchange for Rashaydah support in district (17) where the Rashaydah has 7.4% of the vote. The result was that the Mutayr carried districts (15) and (16) and the Rashaydah carried district (17). This is the only instance where primaries were conducted with pan-tribal considerations.

Interestingly, the Amir of the Awazim tribe was offered a candidacy and refused it, choosing to run for the candidacy in the primary. He did run and lost to the incumbent. This incident shows that at least among this tribe, democracy works, for an Amir ran for the right to represent the tribe and lost (*al-Mujtama'* 1-29-1985).

One social result of the primaries, and to a large extent, of the electoral process in Kuwait, is that it allows the tribes to use tribal ideology to solidify their membership and provide their members with a meaningful group identity that relates to the formal political process and structure. In addition, it allows tribal members to relate to the state through symbols which are tribal, yet using modern state apparatuses, parliamentary elections and primaries. This is true participation and an excellent example of using indigenous symbols and structures to fit modern concepts and processes. The state not only tolerates tribalism, it welcomes, encourages, and nurtures it. Tribalism not only fits the ideology upon which the state is built, it is also used by the government to maintain a level of equilibrium between the major segments of the social structure.

Two Kuwaiti writers on the elections, Abd al-Rida Asiri and Kamal al-Manufi (1986:129) assert that one encouraging outcome of the 1985 elections was that a number of tribal deputies were young, progressive, and educated. This is a result of tribal primaries, which allowed the tribes to put their best qualified candidates forward and prevent its members from wasting their votes on a large number of unqualified candidates (*al-Mujtama* 1-29-1985; *al-Qabas* 12-27-1984).

Alliances and Political Groups in the 1985 Election

The 1985 election was significant for three reasons. First, the elections of 1981 came after a five-year hiatus. Having an election after that disruption provided for continuity and expressed a measure of stability. Secondly, given the Iraqi-Iranian war and the threat of Fundamentalism directed from Iran against Kuwait, having an election at this time was taking the risk of a fundamentalist sweep. The third reason is related to the collapse of the Manakh Stock Market in Kuwait in 1983. This collapse is perceived by the middle class as an attempt by the upper class (the

large merchants and the Sabahs) to curtail and
control the growth of the new middle class. Over
700 such families went into bankruptcy as a result
of the collapse (Markaz 1985; al-Sa'dun 1984).
Their resultant disenchantment, it was feared,
would be expressed at the polls.

Against this background the government
called for new elections for Parliament in 1985.
The most important element in the 1985 elections
was the new election districts of 1981. Redistricting had been done in order to enhance the position of the tribal groups since the fundamentalists, especially those allied with Iran, could no
longer be counted upon to be friendly with the
government. Another reason for the government's
desire to the enhance the position of the tribal
groups was the disenchantment of a large portion
of the urbanites due to events surrounding the
collapse of the Manakh Stock Market.

The 1985 elections had four distinct political currents: Islamic Sunna, Islamic Shia, Liberal and Tribal. Note that by 1985 the Islamic coalition had collapsed and the Shia and Sunnis
represented separate political currents; hence increasing the number of important political groupings from three to four.[7]

I. The most important Islamic current is
Tayyarat Islamiyah Sunna. The major sub-group in
this coalition is Jam'iyat al-Islah al-Ijtima'i,
The Society for Social Reform (SSR). This group
draws its support from the lower middle class, the
petite bourgeois. It is closely related to the
Islamic Brotherhood. Some of its members are
tribesmen such as Mubarak al-Dawilah, an engineer,
who is a member of the Rashaydah tribe. He receives support from his tribe as well from young
professionals and fundamentalists. Other professionals in this group are Dr. Abdallah al-Nafisi
and Dr. Adil al-Subayh, Jamal al-Kandari, Jassim
al-'Awn and Muhammad F. Jifidan (another member of
the Rashaydah tribe.)

The second sub-group is Jam'iyat Ihya' al-Tu-
rath, Society for the Revivication of Heritage
(SRH). The leader of this group, Khalid al-Sultan
belongs to the Janay'at urban merchant family.
The group is related to the Salafiyah Movement.

The third sub-group is Murashahun Islamiyun Mustaqilum, Independent Islamic Candidates (IIC). This group put forward candidates who were founders of (SRH) but are now in sharp disagreement with them.

II. The second major Islamic current is al-Tajamu'at al-Islamiyah al-Shi'iyah, the Shia Islamic Conglomerate (SIC). The Shia in Kuwait make up about 20% of the electorate. Until 1981, they controlled 20% of the Parliament. In 1981, their control was reduced to a mere 8%. This was due to dividing and reorganizing the election districts where they were a majority such as old districts al-Sharq, al-Qadisiyah, al-Da'iyah, al-Rumaythiyah, and Hawalli. In addition a sudden increase in the number of candidates who are Shia caused them to split their vote.

The first Shia sub-group is Jam'iyat al-Thaqafah al-Ijtima'iyah, the Society of Social Culture (SSC). They openly oppose the Kuwaiti regime and ally themselves openly with the Kuwaiti Liberal/Left. They also oppose primaries.

The second sub-group is al-Lujnah al-Wataniyah, the National Committee (NC). These are Shia who have liberal leanings, and ally themselves with the Kuwaiti Liberal/Left.

The third sub-group is Lujnat al-Wajaha, the Committee of Notables (CN). This group was formed to encourage the isolation of radical Shia through conducting primary elections. Members of this group, as the name Wajaha suggests, are well-to-do merchants opposed to fundamentalism and allied with the Kuwaiti establishment.

III. The third major current is al-Tayyarat al-Liberaliyah, the Liberal Currents (LC). In Kuwait the Liberals and the Left are indistinquishable and the terms are often used interchangeably. This group came into being in the 1950s and 1960s and dominated political activity in the country. As stated earlier, the Islamic and tribal groups used to contain the Liberal/Left. These Liberals represent the merchant class, and its educated sons who aspire to more political participation with Liberal-Leftist and pan-Arab Nationalistic goals. During the 1981 elections, only one Liberal/Left candidate, Dr. Khalid al-Wasmi, was elected and Dr. al-Wasmi was elected as a member of the

Awazim tribe which is dominant in the district of
al-Rumaythiyah. All of the other Liberal/Left
candidates were defeated by Fundamentalists and
tribesmen.

The Liberal/Left has three sub-groups--al-Ya-
sar, al-Tajamu' al-Watani, and al-Mutahalifun Ma'
al-Tayyar al-Liberali. Al-Yasar, literally the
Left (L), is composed of the Kuwaiti Communist
Party and the remnants of the Arab Nationalist
Party. The *al-Tali'ah* journal acts as the mouthpiece of this sub-group which today has mainly
students and professors as followers. Their old
middle class backing has waned since 1967 when
they began to openly promote socialist principles.
Dr. Ahmad al-Khatib is considered to be a leader
of this group (*al-Majalah* 2-12-1985).

The second Liberal/Left sub-group is al-Tajamu' al-Watani, the National Gathering (NG).
This group came into being after splitting from
al-Yasar because of its advocation of socialism.
The NG is fiercely nationalistic and liberal (*al-
Majalah* 2-12-1985). This group is sympathetic with
the current political thinking of the Kuwaiti government. Their leader is Jassim al-Qatami, a member of a prominent merchant family.

The third sub-group is al-Mutahalifun Ma'
al-Tayyar al-Liberali, Allies of the Liberal Current (ALC). These are individuals such as Khalid
al-Mas'ud and Dr. Khalid al-Rab'i who support the
Liberal/Left personally without being members of
"formal" groups themselves.

The Liberal/Left, having failed in the 1981
elections, coordinated its efforts in 1985 to insure the success of its members. To this end a
number of its members withdrew from the elections
in order to reduce competition. In addition, and
despite the Liberal/Left's formal opposition to
primaries, a number of its members entered tribal
primaries. For example, Abd Allah al-Rakyan won a
primary as a member of the Ajman tribe and Ahmad
al-Usaymi lost a Utaybah tribal primary.

IV. The fourth important political current
is the Tribal Current, al-Tayyarat al-Qabaliyah.
There are fifteen tribes identified in Kuwait:
al-Awazim, Ajman, Aniza, Shaman, Mutayr, Hajir,
al-Adwan, al-Fudul, al-Dhafiir, al-Dawasir al-
Sib'an, Harb, Sahl, Sulluba, Rashaydah. Members

of these tribes are scattered within fifteen of
the twenty-five election districts. (See Table
6.4). The importance of these tribes in the 1985
elections are discussed throughout this chapter.

The 1985 Campaign

After the primaries the campaign went into
full swing. The issues which became prominent in
the election were in part defined by the currents
and alliances outlined earlier. In general these
issues were reflected in the slogans raised in the
elections. For example, the Liberal/Left had a
slogan "Yes for democracy and social justice."
Other "independent" and tribal candidates had slogans expressing regionalism and parochialism, "Kuwait and its people come first, second and third."
"Kuwait is for all the Kuwaitis." The fundamentalist's slogans refered to Quranic themes: "The
Quran, the Prophet and Hadith," "Your vote is a
testimonial. Do not testify except for the
truth," "I wish nothing but reform to the best of
my ability" (Asiri and al-Manufi 1986:110; *al-Ahram* 2-12-1985).
The vast majority of the candidates had no
platforms or programs. Some justified this by
saying that a platform restricts a candidate, re-
duces his flexibility and makes him a slave of his
words. Others simply published their picture and
name claiming that people know who they are and
where they stand. Yet others claimed that platforms belong to political parties which have no
place in a small country like Kuwait which is after all "one family" (Asiri and al-Manufi
1986:110).
Those who had platforms addressed a wide
spectrum of issues, some of which were oriented
towards their specific districts. The tribal candidates tended to follow this pattern. For example, one advocated the establishment of a mutual
fund for the people of his region to help students, provision of medical care abroad, and the
building of a large guest house (community center)
to conduct weddings and other social gatherings
(Asiri and al-Manufi 1986:110).

Six national issues also surfaced in the campaign: administrative reform, the Manakh Stock Market crisis, citizenship, tribalism, suffrage for women and citizens of the second grade, and foreign affairs.

Administrative Reform. The main issue regarding administrative reform dealt with the Muslim Fundamentalists' call for amending article two of the constitution to call for an Islamic source for all jurisprudence, making the Shari'a the source of all laws constitutionally. The Liberal/ Left opposed this saying that the constitution should not be touched because it guarantees civil liberties. None of the groups ever questioned the overall structure of the Kuwaiti form of government. The Liberal/Left called for the formalization of political parties. The fundamentalists and tribal candidates opposed this. Decentralization was advocated by two candidates but did not generate any response from other candidates.

The Manakh Stock Market Crisis. The collapse of the over-the-counter (informal) stock market (*Suq al-manakh*) in Kuwait in 1982 is locally perceived as the major contributor to the present economic crisis. It is estimated that the losses resulting from the collapse were as high as two thousand million Kuwaiti dinars. Analyses of the cause of the crisis range from those which see it as a purely economic phenomenon (al-Sa'dun 1984) to those which see it as a political/economic event. The later accuse the government and the established merchants of attempting to "put the petit bourgeois" in their place and check their aggressive and somewhat successful upward mobility which was threatening the established merchant families socially, politically, and economically. Whether they posed a real threat or were just a nuisance is debatable (Markaz 1985). It is believed in Kuwait that the real beneficiaries of the crisis were the bedouins who dealt with the market on a short term basis and the big merchants who pulled out in time.

The Liberal/Leftists who represent the social component which was hurt the most by the crisis, advocated economic reform and compensation. The big merchants saw the crisis as one dip in a cycle, no more. The fundamentalists advocated investments in needy Islamic countries (*al-Anba'* 11-27-1984).

Citizenship. Citizenship is intimately related to the tribal policy supported by tribal ideology in Kuwait. The granting of citizenship to only the tribesmen clients of the Sabahs and the denying of it to all other Arabs and non-Arabs is a Kuwaiti fact of life. Since this policy is designed, in part, to provide control over the army and a check on the merchants, the Liberal/Leftists, the Fundamentalists, and the Shia through the use of tribesmen, the issue of citizenship is a political one, one which became a campaign issue. The liberals and the merchants in their attack against the discriminate granting of citizenship to tribesmen never overtly mentioned the political motives of the government. Their attacks were subtle. They complained about granting citizenship to outsiders who become consumers but do not contribute to production. This is a subtle attack on the tribal principle of disdain for manual labor. Others, without ever naming tribesmen specifically, attack the citizenship policy for altering the demographic character of Kuwait. The Liberal/Left also advocated a preference for Arab labor at the expense of non-Arabs, like Koreans, Filipinos, and Indians and the granting of citizenship to such Arabs who lived in the country for a long period of time and granting permanent residence status to others. Members of the Liberal/Left also attacked the policy of granting citizenship of the second degree to "urban" Kuwaitis which denies them the right to vote. These were the old labor class in Kuwait (the new Petit Bourgeoisie), the seamen and other workers, mostly Arabs from Iran, called Hawalla, the same group which suffered from the collapse of the stock market. The tribes were silent on these issues (*al-Anba'* 11-25-1984).

Tribalism. Tribalism and confessionalism were especially important issues during the primaries. Tribal primaries occured as a reaction to the 1981 redistricting and the perceived set backs in the 1981 election by tribesmen. In attacking tribal primaries, the candidates from the *hadaar*, or inner, non-desert districts were also attacking tribalism and implicitly tribal ideology. Such attacks criticized the primaries for promoting tribalism which they consider to be anti-democratic because, they assert, it promotes parochialism and factionalism and prevents the best qualified from being elected. In addition, they asserted that primaries even create conflict between clans of the same tribe. Candidates from the desert and outer districts defended the primaries as a true exercise in democracy which allows members of the districts to "sift" their candidates and express their wishes without having leaders or political bosses do that for them as in the case of political and religious groups (*al-Anba'* 11-22-1984; *al-Watan al-Arabi* 1-4-1985; *al-Ahram* 2-12-1985; *al-Majalah* 2-12-1985).

Suffrage for Women. The issue for women's vote was widely publicized. The Liberal/Left supported it on the basis of true representation, democracy, and equality. Opponents from the religious groups and the tribes argued that women are not ready for the vote because they are not politically "mature" in a "traditional" society such as Kuwait. They said that women should start participating in neighborhood groups, cooperatives and civic organizations before they can participate at the national level. A tribal argument was offered against women's voting rights on the basis that if women were offered the right to vote, it would not alter the results of the elections since these women will vote for the same persons their husbands vote for being members of the same tribe (*al-Anba'* 11-25-1984).

Foreign Affairs. Foreign affairs took a back seat to local matters in the 1985 elections. The Liberal/Left vaguely called for a neutral non-allied foreign policy which would allow for the implementation of the desired local reforms while other tribal and religious candidates mentioned non-Arab labor in Kuwait as a source of social ailments, and a threat to the national character (Asiri and al-Manufi 1986:116).

Candidates expressed their views in a variety of ways using both modern and traditional media. The *hadaar* from the inner non-tribal districts conducted seminars and debates which attracted large audiences where issues were debated. These meetings were for "men only." Some, however, beamed such debates on FM radio waves so women could listen to them in their cars (Asiri and al-Manufi 1986:117).

Kuwaiti radio and television which are government agencies did not cover these debates and rallies. However, the Kuwaiti press had full coverage of the campaign. The press published platforms, conducted interviews and wrote special reports. Some papers like *al-Watan* and *al-Tali'a* were supportive of the Liberal/Left while *al-Mujtama'* magazine, mouthpiece of the Muslim Brotherhood, aired the fundamentalists' views.

Mosques which are attended by Sunni Muslims and Huseyniyat which are attended by Shia Muslims were used by fundamentalists as forums to advocate their positions, attack the Liberal/Leftists, spread religious propaganda and sometimes rumors. In addition, candidates made sure they attended services regularly to be visible (Asiri and al-Manufi 1986:118).

Tribal symbols such as the use of guest houses and feasts (dinner invitations), *dira* (tribal homeland), *rab'* (tribal group), lineage, and *ahl* (tribal extended family) were used by candidates from the outer districts. Tribal dinner parties were attacked by the Liberal/Leftists who contrasted them with their seminars as the difference between the "nourishment of guts" to the "nourishment of the mind" (Asiri and al-Manufi 1986:119).

There were several reports in the press of attempts by some candidates to buy votes. One candidate was reported to have allocated one million dinars to buy 500 votes. This was attacked by the Liberal/Left as well as the religious press. The Ulama issued a *fatwa* declaring it a sin. The Parliament debated it and several bills were proposed making it a crime.

A new campaign phenomenon emerged in the 1985 election called *al-Muftah al-Intikhabi*, the election key. These were persons with wide social and economic contacts who acted as campaign managers for candidates, "opening" the gates for them to reach certain families, tribes and other social groups. These people played an important role in this tribal society where patron-client relations are valuable and where face to face contacts are of the essence (Asiri and al-Manufi 1986:121).

The 1985 Parliament

The 1985 election resulted in a major come-back for the Liberal/Left with the election of thirteen deputies. A number of things contributed to their success. They reduced the number of candidates in districts where they had considerable support by convincing their supporters to withdraw to prevent splitting the vote and to allow for the use of the one-eyed vote. They also entered candidates in districts where their support was small and they had very little chance of winning in order to provide public exposure for their views. Another reason for their success is their stress on debating the issues and the sympathy they drew from the lower middle class *hadaar* on the issue of Suq al-Manakh. In addition the Iraqi-Iranian war provided a scare in Kuwait which was used against the Fundamentalists.

The Fundamentalists elected only six members. Their attacks on the Liberal/Left in their paper *al-Mujtama'* backfired when prominent professors from the university counter-attacked in *al-Watan* and *al-Tali'a* pointing to the "fallacies" of their attack as "tashhir", an Islamic term which means malicious rumors. One interesting result of the elections is that in three districts—Hawalli (8), Kayfan (7) and Fayha' (6)—one winner was a Fundamentalist and the other a Liberal/Left candidate.

The Shia elected only four candidates, two of whom were from the A'yan, a non-Khumayni and pro-ruling family group. The result of their poor showing is not only due to redistricting but also to the fact that a large number of candidates competed, thus splitting the vote. The merchants had ten winners. Many of these merchants are nationalists who tend to ally themselves with the Liberal/Left on certain issues regarding civil liberties and in opposing the tribal pressure from the outer districts.

I identify twenty-one tribal winners although after the election a group of twenty-seven deputies formed a coalition called al-Tajamu' al-Arabi al-Islami (the Arab Islamic Coalition) which stressed demands emanating from the outer, desert tribal districts. These districts are deprived

compared with the inner urban-*hadaar* districts,
and the coalition's demands included better services, development projects, and open admissions to
the university. One frustrating dimension of the
tribal element for this author is that although
Kuwaiti writers and journalists openly deal with
the tribal issue, pro and con, they never published a complete list of tribal candidates or
winners. Names are mentioned here and there but
one never sees a comprehensive list. One paper
reporting on the "coalition of the 27" mentioned
some names but did not give a complete list (*al-
Tali'ah* 3-3-1985). When the election results were
reported the Liberal/Left, the Shia, and the Fundamentalists were all identified by name, but the
merchants and the tribal winners were not. There
are two possible explanations for this. First, in
a small society everybody knows who they are.
Secondly, since tribalism is an ideology guiding
the actions of the government and permeating all
aspects of culture and society in a subtle manner,
it cannot be acknowledged formally as an ideology
nor articulated by government officials as such.
In this light tribal lists are left vague and uns-
poken. The "coalition of 27" collapsed after the
government threatened to treat them as an illegal
political party on constitutional grounds (*al-Siyasa* 1-27-1985 and 12-15-1985).

The reason for the tribal success in the
1985 election is due, for the most part, to redistricting. Tribal primaries did not gain more
votes for the tribesmen than they had in 1981, but
it solidified their position showing that tribal
districts were something special not only because
they were the only ones who had the structural
means to hold primaries, but also because of the
special attention the media paid to the primaries
and the controversy they generated (*al-Mujtama'*
1-15-1985; *al-Majalah* 2-12-1985; *al-Ahram* 2-12-1985;
al-Watan 2-19-1985; *al-Anba'* 12-11-1985). Table 6.5
summarizes the tribal membership in Parliament
from 1963-1985.

Overall the voters returned twenty-two deputies from the 1981 parliament (44%), hence the new
parliament is 56% new-comers. This figure is in
line with previous elections. Seven districts had
completely new deputies. These were mixed tribal
and *hadaar* districts while fourteen districts had

a partial change and only four returned all previous deputies. The new parliament is characterized as being 70% conservative and 30% Liberal/Left (*al-Watan* 2-21-1985).

The social composition of the new parliament had the following profile: the ages of the deputies ranged from thirty-one to sixty-one years old with an average age of forty-three. As for the educational background of the deputies, 46% of the deputies are college graduates compared to 34% of the previous parliament. Overall, the new parliament is better educated than the five previous ones. The new parliament also has a higher proportion of professionals than the previous ones. Sixty percent are self-employed, 8 percent are university professors, and 10 percent are professionals. Finally, 70 percent of the deputies are socially active as members of cooperatives, clubs, and local councils (*al-Anba'* 2-27-1985).

Conclusions

The 1985 elections in Kuwait produced a parliament reflective of the social structure as designed by the Kuwaiti authorities through their policies of tribal settlement, migration, labor and paternalism. Despite the fact that the government did not directly interfere in the electoral process (there were no press reports nor any other kind of reports to this effect (Asiri and al-Manufi 1986:133), the outcome was in line with the government's desired results. It produced a parliament in which the tribal element contains the merchants who seek more power from the rulers, the Liberal/Left which seeks social and economic equality, and the Fundamentalists who seek an Islamic government. To be able to achieve such a balance without direct interference in the electoral process is testimonial to the maturity and stability of the Kuwaiti political system. This stability is also due to the sophistication of the Kuwaiti rulers in their use of an ideology which is deeply rooted in the body politic of Kuwait and the Gulf in general. The relationship between the desert and the city is an age-old one in the region. This relationship has been mastered through

182

the application of a policy derived from an ideology that all the populace, whether rich or poor,
urban or desert, noble or vassal, can understand
and relate to. This ideology was used as the
foundation of the Kuwaiti state and later used to
modernize it. Such an ideology has the ability to
provide the symbols, the media, and the rationale
for social, political, economic, and cultural actions which are all-inclusive, meaningful and indigenous. It can provide modern western materials
and even institutions (elections and primaries)
and filter them through a native membrane to ren-
der them familiar, acceptable and even tribal.
The Kuwaiti authorities, having a full grasp of
this ideology, laid the foundations for the stability of their state through re-settlement policies, social services, education and patronage,
year after year and then let election results re-
flect a balance which they deem healthy and man-
ageable. Their policies work because, though
evolving over the last one hundred years, they are
consistent, and comprehensive. Their people understand them and relate to them. What makes tribal ideology even more powerful and pervasive be-
sides being truly Arab, is the fact that it is
never formally articulated, stated, written down
or even openly criticized. It is just there, permeating every action, thought or process which is
of sociopolitical significance. Only the states
of the Arab Gulf and maybe Jordan and Morocco have
such indigenous ideologies. No wonder they are
the most stable countries in the Middle East in
terms of the durability of their regimes. To be
able to hold elections with tribal primaries is a
sign of stability, confidence and maturity. The
Kuwaitis can afford to do that because of the
ideology of their state.

Epilogue

During the month of June 1986 a crisis atmosphere prevailed in Kuwait between Parliament and the government. This crisis ended in the collective resignation of the Council of Ministers on July 1, 1986. Two days later on July 3, 1986, the Amir suspended Parliament and imposed restrictions on the press. The immediate reason behind these actions was the persistance of the members of Parliament in calling in ministers for questioning. On the day the Council of Ministers resigned, the Minister of Communications was supposed to testify. The Council of Ministers accused members of Parliament of going far beyond legitimate questioning. They asserted that the real intent of the questioning was to cause embarrassment to the ministers and cause them to resign. The Amir asserted that the questioning was meant to "settle old scores and was not looking forward to the future."

The war between Iraq and Iran touched upon Kuwait directly in the form of bombings and assassination attempts carried out by members of pro-Iranian groups. On April 24, 1985 the editor of *al-Siyasa* was wounded in a bombing of the offices of his newspaper. On May 25, 1985, the motorcade of the Amir of Kuwait was attacked and the Amir was wounded. On June 17, 1985, the air fields in Ahmadi were bombed and burned, and on June 25, 1985, two popular seaside cafes were bombed.

The economy continued to stagnate and a state of siege prevailed. The Amir justified suspending Parliament on the grounds that political bickering between the members of Parliament and the ministers threatened the security of the state under the prevailing difficult circumstances (*al-Siyasa* 7-2-1986; 7-3-1986; 7-4-1986).

184

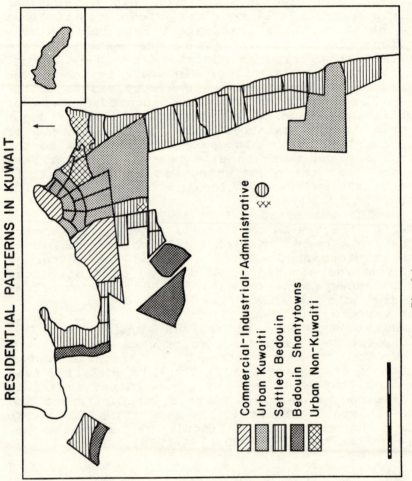

RESIDENTIAL PATTERNS IN KUWAIT

Commercial-Industrial-Administrative

Urban Kuwaiti

Settled Bedouin

Bedouin Shantytowns

Urban Non-Kuwaiti

Fig. 6.1

Table 6.1

Kuwait's Old Voting Districts and Social Groups

1. Sharq - Shia
2. Qiblah - Sunni merchants
3. al-Shuwaykh - Tribes: Shammar, Dafiir, Ajman,
                          Aniza
4. al-Shamiyah - Tribes: Mutayr, Rashaydah
5. Kayfan - Mixed Merchants and Utaybah Tribe
6. al-Qadisiyah - Liberal Young Sunna
                          Professionals
7. al-Dasma - Shia and Sunna (evenly split)
8. Hawalli - Small, Liberal, Sunna Merchants
9. al-Salmiyah - Awazim Tribe
10. al-Ahmadi - Tribes: Ajman, Awazim, Fudul

186

Table 6.2

Kuwait's New and Old Election Districts

Name	1981-present	1961-1975
Sharq (Kuwait City)	1	1
al-Shuwaykh	2	3*
al-Qiblah	3	2
al-Dasma	4	7
al-Qadisiyah	5	6
al-Shamiyah	6	4
Kayfan	7	5
Hawalli	8	8
al-Rawda	9	
al-'Addayliyah	10	
al-Khaldiyah	11	
al-Salmiyah	12	9
al-Rumaythiyah	13	
Abraq Khaytan	14	
al-Furwaniyah	15	
al-Umariyah	16	
Jaliib al-Shuyukh	17	
al-Sulaybikhat	18	
al-Jahra al-Jadidah	19	
al-Jahra al-Qadimah	20	
al-Ahmadi	21	10
al-Riqah	22	
al-Sabahiyah	23	
al-Fahahiil	24	
Um al-Hayman (al-Bar)	25	

* Al-Ghazali (1985) refers to old district (3) as
al-Mirqab, old district (4) as al-Fayha, and old
district (7) as al-Da'iyah.

Table 6.3

Members of Parliament 1981 (al-Ghazali 1985)

Name	Affiliation
Fayiz H. al-Bughayli	Rashaydah
Falah M. al-Hajraf	Ajman
Faysal B. al-Darish	Mutayr
Faysal J. al-Qadibi	
Mubarak F.R. al-Fahman	Awazim
Mubarak A. al-Dabus	Fudul
Muhammad A. al-Rashiid	
Muhammad H. Badr	Merchant
Muhammad H. al-Barrak	Mutayr
Muhammad S. al-Murshid	
Muhammad D.A. al-Qahs	
Murdi A. al-Udhayna	Awazim
Mraykhan S. Saqr	Mutayr
Mushari J. al-Anjari	
Mutlaq M. al-Shilaymi	Dafiir
Mutlaq M. al-Mus'ud	
Hamud N. al-Yahri	
Nasir Sarkhawa	
Nayif A. Ibn Rumayih	Mutayr
Hadi Hayif al-Hawilah	Ajman
Hadil S. al-Jalawi	Awazim
Yusif A. al-Shahiin	
Isa al-Mazidi	
Muhammad Y. al-Adasani	Merchant
Ahmad A. al-Sa'dun	Merchant
Ahmad F. al-Takhiim	
Badr A. al-Mudif	
Yasir K. al-Yasir	
Jassim M. al-Saqr	Merchant
Jassim M. al-Khurafi	Merchant
Jassim M. al-Awn	
Hazzam F. al-May'	Awazim
Hummud H. al-Rumi	Merchant
Khalid S.B. Isa	Fundamentalist
Khalid al-Ajran	Ajman
Khalid A. al-Mus'ib	Rashaydah
Khalid al-Wasmi	Awazim
Khalaf D. al-Anizi	Aniza
Khalifah T. al-Jari	Ajman

TABLE 6.3 cont.

Rashid S. al-Jihaylan	Awazim
Salim A. al-Hammad	Awazim
Salih Y. al-Faddalah	Merchant
Sayyah Sh. Ibn Shaykhah	Aniza
Ayid A. al-Khmayshi	Awazim
Abd al-Razzaq A. al-Sani'	
Abd al-Kariim H. al-Jihaydali	Rashaydah
Abd al-Muhsin Yusif Jamal	Fundamentalist
Adnan S. Abd al-Samad	Fundamentalist
Isa M. al-Shahiin	Fundamentalist

Those who are not identified are
hadaar.

Table 6.4

Tribal Concentration in Tribal Voting Districts

District	Reg. Voters	Tribe	Reg. Voters	District %
8. Hawalli	3295	Awazim	300	(9.1%)
12. al-Salmiyah	1618	Awazim	1,050	(64.89%)
13. al-Rumaythiyah	3809	Awazim	1,600	(42.00%)
14. Abraq Khaytan	2215	Utaybah	620	(27.9%)
15. al-Furwaniyah	2752	Rashaydah	1,252	(45.49%)
		Adwan	150	(5.4%)
		Mutayr	400	(14.5%)
		Awazim	150	(5.4%)
16. al-Umariyah	2811	Rashaydah	653	(22.5%)
		Mutayr	545	(19.3%)
		Awazim	150	(5.3%)
		Adwan	130	(4.6%)
		Utaybah	100	(3.5%)
17. Jaliib al-Shuyukh	2004	Mutayr	1,300	(64.8%)
		Rashaydah	150	(7.4%)
		Adwan	73	(3.6%)
18. al-Sulaybikhat	2406	Awazim	320	(13.3%)
19. al-Jahra al-Jadidah	2006	Aniza	300	(14.95%)
		Dafiir	300	(14.95%)
		Rashaydah	263	(13.1%)
20. al-Jahra al-Qadimah	3105	Aniza	560	(18.00%)
		Ajman	450	(14.49%)
		Dafiir	350	(11.27%)
21. al-Ahmadi	3471	Ajman	980	(28.33%)
		Awazim	300	(8.64%)
		Utaybah	350	(10.00%)
22. al-Riqah	2264	Awazim	650	(28.7%)
		Ajman	600	(26.5%)
		Mutayr	415	(18.3%)
23. al-Sabahiyah	3208	Ajman	1,149	(35.8%)
		Awazim	1,100	(34.2%)
24. al-Fahahiil	2054	Awazim	400	(19.4%)
		Hajir Qahtan	384	(18.69%)
25. Um al-Hayman	1556	Awazim	800	(51.4%)

Based on primary election estimates *al-Anba'* 11-22-1984.

TABLE 6.5

**Members of Parliament by Tribal Group, 1963-1985
(Estimates)**

	1963	1967	1971	1975	1981	1985
Adwan	1	1	1	0	0	0
Ajman	3	1	7	7	4	4
Aniza	0	0	1	2	2	3
Awazim	6	7	5	5	9	6
Dafiir	0	0	0	0	1	1
Fadawira	0	0	1	1	0	0
Fudul	3	1	0	0	1	0
Hajir	0	0	0	0	0	0
Mutayr	2	3	5	2	4	3
Rashaydah	3	1	1	3	3	5
Shammar	2	1	0	0	0	0
Utaybah	0	4	3	3	0	2
Total	20	19	24	23	24	21

Notes

[1] Oil was discovered in 1938 following an
agreement signed in 1934 between the Amir and the
Kuwait Oil Company (a joint venture between the
Anglo Persion Oil Company and Gulf). World War II
prevented its development, but following the post-
war resumption of operations, oil revenues rose
rapidly, from $760,000 in 1946, the first year of
exports, to over $8 billion by the early eighties
(Crystal 1985:4).

[2] The heir apparent is selected by the Sabah
family council and is always, by virtue of that
position, Prime Minister. See Crystal 1985:29-31
for a discussion of the alternating system between
the Jabir and Salim lines.

[3] See Dickson 1949, Mahgoub 1974, Hamza 1933,
Cole 1975, and Sweet 1964, 1965 for a description
of the social structure prevailing in Eastern Arabia as manifested in Kuwait before the discovery
of oil.

[4] The members of Jam'iyat al-Islah, are read-
ily identified in Kuwait by the fact that they
wear their *dishdashas* (robes) above the ankle, a
length considered short by Gulf standards. Members of this group wear a short *dishdasha* in order
to keep it from coming in contact with dirt,
thereby maintaining the state of purity (*tuhur*)
necessary for prayer.

[5] Three of the over sixty members of the Wahhabi *Ikhwan* who occupied the holy mosque in Mecca
in 1980 and were subsequently beheaded by the Saudi government were Kuwaitis (Abu Dhur
1980:277-280).

[6] Representation from specific tribal groups
changed. The Ajman, who are maternally related to
an important group of the Sabah, the leader of
which had aspirations for the post of Amir, increased from three in 1963 to seven in 1975. The
Utaybah who held no seats in 1963 won two seats in
1975. The number of parliamentary seats held by
the Awazim and Rashaydah, two non-*asiil*, *arab daar*
tribes remained the same. These are old loyal te-
nants of the Sabahs.

[7] The term "political currents" is used to
correspond with the Arabic term *"tayyarat"* (*al-Mujtama'* 1-15-1985).

Appendix A

MEMBERS OF THE LEGISLATIVE ASSEMBLY IN KUWAIT 1963-1976 BY ETHNICITY AND TRIBAL AFFILIATION (NAFISI 1978)

DISTRICT I	AFFILIATION
Session I 1963-1967	
Ibrahiim Khraybit	Shia
Hassan Jawhar Hayyat	Shia
Yusif Sayyid Hashim al-Rifa'i	Sunna
Ahmad Sayyid 'Abid al-Musawi	Shia
Muhammad Hussain Qabazid	Shia
Session II 1967-1971	
Ibrahiim Khraybit	Shia
Hassan Jawhar Hayyat	Shia
Yusif Sayyid Hashim al-Rifa'i	Sunna
Isa 'Abd Allah Bahman	Shia
Mansur Musa al-Mazidi	Shia
Session III 1971-1975	
Ibrahiim Khraybit	Shia
Hassan Jawhar Hayyat	Shia
Yusif Sayyid Hashim al-Rifa'i	Sunna
Isa 'Abd Allah Bahman	Shia
Ahmad Sayyid 'Abid al-Musawi	Shia
Session IV 1975-1976	
Ibrahiim Khraybit	Shia
Isma'il Ali Dashti	Shia
Habiib Hassan Hayyat	Shia
Khalid Khalaf	Shia
Isa 'Abd Allah Bahman	Shia

This district is composed of the following quarters (*furjan* or *ahya'*): al-Sharq, al-Hassawiyah, al-Rashaydah, al-'Alaywah, al-Mutran, al-Musayl, al-Sawabir, al-Baloush. It is estimated that 85%-95% of the inhabitants are Shia and are of Persian origin. The Arab Shia are from al-Hassa, Bahrain and al-Qatiif. The Baloush and Rashaydah are Sunna.

DISTRICT II

AFFILIATION

Session I 1963-1967

Ali Ibrahiim al-Mawwash
Sulayman al-Duwayk
Humud Zayd al-Khalid
Abd al-Aziiz al-Saqr
Rashid al-Farhan

Hadaar, Utaybah

Session II 1967-1971

Ibrahiim Muhammad al-Maylim
Sulayman al-Duwayk
Abd al-Aziiz Ibrahiim al-Falayj
Ali Ibrahiim al-Mawwash
Ghanim al-'Umayri

Hadaar, Utaybah

Session III 1971-1975

Ibrahiim Muhammad al-Maylim
Salim Khalid al-Marzuq
Sulayman al-Duwayk
Ali Ibrahiim al-Mawwash
Ali Muhammad Thunayyan al-Ghanim

Hadaar, Utaybah

Session IV 1975-1976

Jassim al-Saqr
Jassim al-Qatami
Salim Khalid al-Marzuq
Ahmad al-Sa'dun
Jassim al-Khurafi

This district is composed of the following quarters: Qibla, al-Mirqab, al-Salhiya, al-Shuwaykh.
The inhabitants of this district are predominantly
of Najd origin and are Sunna.

DISTRICT III	AFFILIATION

Session I 1963-1967

Bandar Sa'ad al-Laafi	Shammar
Hammad Mubarak al-'Ayyar	Adwan
Khalid Salih al-Ghnaym	
Abd Allah Fahd al-Laafi	Shammar
Falah Mubarak al-Hajraf	Ajman

Session II 1967-1971

Hammad Mubarak al-'Ayyar	Adwan
Khalid Salih al-Ghnaym	
Falah Mubarak al-Hajraf	Ajman
Laafi Fahd al-Laafi	Shammar
Salih Abd al-Wahhab al-Rumi	

Session III 1971-1975

Hammad Mubarak al-'Ayyar	Adwan
Falah Muhammad al-Hajraf	Ajman
Muhammad Dayf Allaf al-Jahas	'Aniza
Nasir Muhammad al-Sayir	Mutayr
Khalid Salih al-Ghnaym	

Session IV 1975-1976

Abd Allah Fahd al-Laafi (died)	Shammar
Falah Mubarak al-Hajraf	Ajman
Khalid Salih al-Ghnaym	
Yusif al-Majiim al-Shallal	'Aniza
Muhammad Dayf Allah al-Jahas	'Aniza

This district is composed of the following quarters: al-Jahra'; al-Sulaybikhat; al-Dawha. Al-Jahra' is inhabited mainly by members of the following tribes: Ajman, Shammar, 'Aniza, and some Sulluba. al-Sulaybikhat is inhabited by members of the Hirshan and the following sections of the Sulluba: al-Majid, al-Badhaali, and al-Hulaylat. al-Dawha is inhabited by members of the tribes Shammar, 'Aniza, Mutayr, Awazim and al-Rashaydah.

DISTRICT IV   AFFILIATION

Session I 1963-1967

Abbas Habiib Munawir	Rashaydah
Muhammad Hammad al-Barrak	Mutayr
Yusif Khalid al-Mukhlid	Mutayr
Khalid Nazzal al-Mu'sib	Rashaydah
Mudhi al-Nazzal al-Mu'sib	Rashaydah

Session II 1967-1971

Abbas Habiib Munawir	Rashaydah
Muhammad Hammad al-Barrak	Mutayr
Yusif Khalid al-Mukhlid	Mutayr
Abd al-Kariim Hilal al-Jahaydali	Mutayr
Khalid Isa al-Salih	Mutayr

Session III 1971-1975

Abbas Habiib Munawir	Rashaydah
Muhammad Hammad al-Barrak	Mutayr
Yusif Khalid al-Mukhlid	Mutayr
Abd al-Kariim Hilal al-Jahaydali	Mutayr
Ghanim Ali al-Jumhour	Mutayr

Session IV 1975-1976

Abbas Habiib Munawir	Rashaydah
Muhammad Hammad al-Barrak	Mutayr
Yusif Khalid al-Mukhlid	Mutayr
Faisal al-Dawiish	Mutayr
Nasir al-Hammad	Rashaydah

This district is composed of the quarters of al-Furwaniyah and Jaliib al-Shuyukh. It is inhabited by members of two tribes: al-Rashaydah and Mutayr.

198

DISTRICT V   AFFILIATION

Session I 1963-1967

Jassim Abd al-Azziz al-Qatami
Khalid Mas'ud al-Fahayd   Ajman
Rashid Salih al-Tawhid
Khalil Ibrahiim al-Muzayin   Sunna'
Ya'qub Yusif al-Hamaydi

Session II 1967-1971

Khalid Muhammad al-Tahous   Utaybah
Khalaf al-Utaybi   Utaybah
Khalil Ibrahiim al-Muzayin   Sunna'
Nasir Sanhat al-'Usaymi   Utaybah-Burqa
Ahmad al-Khalifi

Session III 1971-1975

Jassim Isma'il al-Yassin   Fawadira
Badir Dahi al-'Ujayl
Khalid al-Mas'ud al-Fahayd   Ajman
Muhammad Abd al-Muhsin al-Usaymi   Utaybah-Burqa
Nasir Sanhat al-'Usaymi   Utaybah-Burqa

Session IV 1975-1976

Badir al-Jabri   Utaybah-Burqa
Khalid al-Mas'ud   Ajman
Abd al-Razzaq al-Sana'   Sunna'
Khalif al-Utaybi   Utaybah
Nasir al-'Usaymi   Utaybah-Burqa

This district is composed of the quarters of Kayfan, Khaytan and al-Khaldiyah. Kayfan is inhabited by urban (*hadaar*) Sunnis who came from the Qiblah quarter in the old city of Kuwait. Khaytan is
inhabited by members of the tribes of Ajman, Utaybah and Mutayr. Al-Khaldiyah is inhabited by *hadaar* (Sunna) who came from the old quarter of al-
Mirqab and few Shia.

DISTRICT VI   AFFILIATION

Session I 1963-1967

Abd al-Baqi Abd Allah al-Nouri
Ahmad Khalid al-Fawzan
Hammad Abd al-Muhsin al-Mushari
Abd al-Azziz al-Ali al-Khalid
Sulayman Ahmad al-Haddad (resigned and replaced by)
Ali al-Umar

Session II 1967-1971

Ahmad Abd al-Latiif al-Abd al-Jaliil
Ahmad Mayif al-Khalifi
Rashid Ibrahiim Isma'il
Mubarak Abd al-Azziz al-Hassawi
Yusif Abd al-Azziz al-Wazzan

Session III 1971-1975

Ahmad Yusif al-Nafisi	Pro. Democrat
Rashid Abd Allah al-Farhan	Pat. Alliance
Muhammad al-Rashiid	
Abd Allah Muhammad al-Nibari	Pro. Democrat
Mubarak Abd al-Azziz al-Hassawi	

Session IV 1975-1976

Muhammad Habiib	Kandari
Abd al-Rahman al-Awadi	Awadiyah
Abd Allah al-Nibari	Pro. Democrat
Rashid Abd al-Allah al-Farhan	Pat. Alliance
Muhammad Ahmad Rashiid	

This district is composed of the following quar-
ters: al-Qadisiyah, al-Fayha', al-Nuzha, and al-
Mansuriya. The inhabitants of this district are
Sunna of Najd origin with the exception of al-Qad-
isiyah where a number of Kanadira (former water
carrier caste of Persian origin) and some of the
Awadiyah (Arab Shia from the Eastern shore of the
Gulf) live.

DISTRICT VII   AFFILIATION

Session I 1963-1967

Hummud Yusif al-Nisf	Sunna
Zayd al-Kadhimi	Shia
Khalid Ahmad al-Mudif	Sunna
Abd Allah Mushari al-Rawdan	Sunna
Muhammad Hussain Qabazid	Shia

Session II 1967-1971

Ibrahiim Tahir al-Mutawi'	Sunna
Jassim al-Qattan	Shia
Zayd al-Kadhmi	Shia
Abd al-Latiif al-Kadhimi	Shia
Abd Allah Ali Dashti	Shia

Session III 1971-1975

Badir Abd Allah al-Mudif	Sunna
Khalid Mushari al-Rawdan	Sunna
Abd al-Latiif al-Kadhimi	Shia
Yusif Salih al-Rumi	Sunna
Abd al-Muttalib al-Kadhimi	Shia

Session IV 1975-1976

Abd al-Muttalib al-Kadhimi	Shia
Hussain Ma'rifi	Shia
Abd Allah al-Wazzan	Shia
Jassim al-Qattan	Shia
Hussain Makki Jum'a	Shia

This district is composed of the quarters of al-
Dasma, al-Da'iyah, and the island of Faylaka. Al-
Dasma is composed mainly of Awadiyah and Kanadira,
al-Da'iyahis inhabited mainly by Persian Shia
(Ja'fariya). The island of Faylaka is inhabited
by Hawalla and a minority of Persian Shia.

DISTRICT VIII   AFFILIATION

Session I 1963-1967

Ahmad Zayd al-Sarhan
Ahmad Muhammad al-Khatib   Pro. Democrat
Sami Ahmad Munayis   Pro. Democrat
Sulayman Khalid al-Mutawi'   Pro. Democrat
Ali Salih al-Faddalah

Session II 1967-1971

Ahmad Zayd al-Sarhan
Khalid Abd al-Latiif al-Muslim
Abd al-Azziz Fahd al-Masa'id
Ali Salih al-Faddalah
Nasir Ali al-Mu'ayli

Session II 1971-1975

Ahmad Muhammad al-Khatib
Abd al-Azziz Fahd al-Masa'id
Ali Abd Allah al-Habashi
Ali Salih al-Faddalah
Sami al-Munayis

Session IV 1975-1976

Ahmad Muhammad al-Khatib
Abd al-Azziz Fahd al-Masa'id
Ali Abd Alah al-Habashi
Jasi al-Jasir
Sami al-Munayis

This district contains the quarters of Hawalli,
al-Nugra, al-Jabriya, and al-Udayliya. The Kuwaiti inhabitants of Hawalli originate from the Qiblah quarter of the old city. They are *hadaar* Sunna. In addition Hawalli contains members of the
tribes of Rashaydah and Awazim and a small minority of Shia. Al-Nugra is mainly inhabited by non-
Kuwaitis. Al-Udayliya is mainly inhabited by *hadaar* (Sunna) and small minority of Shia.
Al-Jabriya is inhabited by a mixture of tribal minorities.

DISTRICT IX	AFFILIATION

Session I 1963-1967

Khalaf Khalifah al-Hamidah	Awazim
Salim Ghanim al-Haris	Awazim
Ali Thunayan al-Uḍhaynah	Awazim
Muhammad Wasmi al-Sidayran	Awazim
Mardi Abd Allah al-Udhaynah	Awazim

Session II 1967-1971

Jam'an al-Harithi	Awazim
Rashid Awad al-Juwaysiri	Awazim
Ali Thunayan al-Udhaynah	Awazim
Muhammad Wasmi al-Sedayran	Awazim
Mardi Abd Allah al-'Udhaynah	Awazim

Session III 1971-1975

Jam'an al-Harithi	Awazim
Rashid Awad al-Juwaysiri	Awazim
Falih Hummud Suwaylih	Awazim
Muhammad Wasmi al-Sudayran	Awazim
Mardi Abd Allah al-Udhaynah	Awazim

Session IV 1975-1976

Jam'an al-Harithi	Awazim
Rashid Awad al-Juwaysiri	Awazim
Muhammad Wasmi al-Sudayran	Awazim
Mardi Abd Allah al-Udhaynah	Awazim
Salim Hammad	Awazim

This district is composed of the quarters of al-Salmiyah, al-Bida' and al-Rumaythiyah. Al-Salmiyah is mainly inhabited by non-Kuwaitis, however, the Kuwaiti inhabitants are predominantly from the tribe of Awazim followed by small numbers of Mutayr, Ajman, Dafiir and a small minority of Shia and al-Burayki. Al-Rumaythiyah and al-Bida' are inhabited by *hadaar* Sunna with a small minority of Shia.

DISTRICT X	AFFILIATION

Session I 1963-1967

Hazzam Falih al-Mani'	Awazim
Khalifah Talal al-Jari	Ajman
Ali Ghanim al-Dabbus	Fudul
Nayif Hammad al-Dabbus	Fadoul
Mubarak Abd Allah al-Dabbus	Fudul

Session II 1967-1971

Hazzam Falih al-Mani'	Awazim
Rashid Sayf al-Jihaylan	Awazim
Muflih Sarhan al-Nami	
Falih Hummud Suwaylih	
Mubarak Abd Allah al-Dabbus	Fadoul

Session III 1971-1975

Khalid Ajran Jabir	Ajman
Sa'd Falah Tami	Ajman
Sultan Salman Sultan	Ajman
Abd Allah Hamad al-Hashimi	Ajman
Su'oud Sa'd al-Hamlan	Ajman

Session IV 1975-1976

Sa'd Falah Tami	Ajman
Khalid Ajran Jabir	Ajman
Sultan Salman Sultan	Ajman
Muraykhan Sa'd	Ajman
Hadi Hayif al-Hawilah	Ajman

This district contains the areas of Funtas, al-Ah-
madi, al-Shu'ayba, al-Fahahiil, and al-Munqif.
Al-Funtas is inhabited by *hadaar* of tribal origin.
The other quarters are purely tribal mainly of the
Ajman tribe followed by minorities from Awazim,
Mutayr, Utaybah, Suhoul, Fudul (Dababiis).

Appendix B

Summary of 1981 Redistricting

Old District (1) Sharq, one of the districts with the heaviest Shia concentration, was left intact, but with the new system its representatives were reduced from five to two.

Old District (2) al-Qiblah, with a heavy concentration of Sunni Merchants was divided into three new districts: new district (2) al-Shuwaykh, new district (3) al-Qiblah, and new district (4) al-Dasma with a net gain for the old district (2) of one deputy.

Old District (3) al-Shuwaykh was sub-divided into three separate districts: new district (18) al-Sulaybikhat, (19) al-Jahra al-Jadidah, and (20) al-Jahra al-Qadimah. Each new district had two deputies, thereby increasing the number of deputies from old District (3) by one.

Old District (4) al-Shamiyah was sub-divided into three separate districts: new district (17) Jaliib al-Shuyukh, (15) al-Furwaniyah and, and (16) al-Umariyah.

Old District (5) Kayfan which had a mixed tribal and urban-merchant population was divided into three new districts: new district (14) Abraq Khaytan which is tribal, new district (7) Kayfan left with the Urban-Merchant concentration, and new district (11) al-Khaldiyah with an urban-merchant concentration. The net gain for the old district (5) was one deputy to the merchant segment.

Old District (6) al-Qadisiyah with a young Sunna professsional concentration, was divided into two districts: new district (6) al-Shamiyah and new district (5) al-Qadisiyah. The result was a net loss of one deputy from the old "liberal" district.

Old District (7) al-Dasma remained the same. Old District (8) Hawalli with a heavy liberal concentration, was divided into two new districts: new district (8) Hawalli and new district (10) al--'Addayliyah with a net loss of one deputy for the old liberal district.

Old District (9) al-Salmiyah with a heavy concentration of the Awazim tribe was divided into two new districts: new district (12) al-Salmiyah and new district (13) al-Rumaythiyah with a net loss of the old tribal district by on deputy.

Old District (10) al-Ahmadi, with a heavy tribal concentration was divided into ten new districts as follows: New Districts - (21) al-Ahmadi, (24) al-Fahahiil, (25) Um al-Hayman, (22) al-Riqah, (23) al-Sabahiyah. The net gain for this old tribal district (10) al-Ahmadi was five deputies.

(Compiled by Gavrielides from Asiri and al-Manufi 1986:98-99, and al-Ghazali 1985)

Appendix C

1985 Candidates by District and Affiliation

Name of Candidate	Affiliation
District I	
Khalid J.S. al-Jmay'am*	Sunna
Ya'qub M.A.H. Hayati*	NC, Shia
Jassim M.A.H. Bu Hamad	Sunna
Khalid A.J. al-Madaf	Sunna
Salim S.A. al-Abd al-Razzaq	Sunna
Adnan Sayyid Abd al-Samad	SSC, Shia
Qassim M.A.A. al-Sarraf	Shia
Mustafa A.Q. Ma'rifi	Shia
District II	
Hammad A.M.A. al-Ju'an	L, Sunna
Subhi A.K. S. al-Ghnaym	Sunna
Ahmad Y.A. al-Nafisi	L, Sunna
Khalid Sultan Bin 'Isa	Merchant, Sunna
District III	
Jassim A.A. Abd al-Qafati	NG/L, Sunna
Jassim M.A.A. al-Khurafi	Sunna
Jassim H.A. al-Saqr	Sunna
Talib A.A.H. Farah	Shia

* The two winning candidates for each district
are listed first.

    NC - National Committee
    L -   Left
    SSC - Society of Social Culture
    CN -   Committee of Notables
    NG -   National Gathering
    SSR - Society for Social Reform
    SRH - Society for the Revivication of Heritage
    IIC - Independent Islamic Candidates

Name of Candidate	Affiliation
District IV	
Abd Allah Y. al-Rumi	Sunna
Nasir A.M.A. al-Rudan	Sunna
Ibrahiim I.I. Isma'il	
Hassan A.A.M. al-Qalaf	Shia
Hussain M. al-Jum'a	CN, Shia
Abd al-Rida A.H. Ali	Shia
Yusif Ali I. al-Mana'i	Sunna
District V	
Abd al-Azziz A.M. al-Mutawi'	SSC, Sunna
Abd Allah S.I. al-Kulaib	IIC, Sunna
Ahmad Y.Y.B. al-Abd Allah	SRH, Sunna
Ja'far J.S. al-Majdi	Shia
Hawqal A.A. al-Hawqal	
Saud A.A. al-Ramadan	Shia
Abd al-Ali N.A. Abd al-Aali	Shia
Abd al-Azziz Ali A. al-Andali *	CN, Shia
Abd al-Muhsin Y.A.I. Jamal	SSC, Shia
Ali S.J.S.A.S.A. al-Nasir	Shia
Muhammad H.H. Badr	Shia
District VI	
Hummud H.A. al-Rumi	SSR, Sunna
Mushari J.M. al-'Anjari	L, Sunna
Rashid A.A. al-Farhan	L
Abd Allah M.A. al-Nibari	L
Muhammad D.H.A. al-Barazi	Sunna
Muhammad A.I.al-'As'usi	Sunna
District VII	
Faisal A. al-Sana'	L, Sunna
Jassim M.S. al-Awn	SRH, Sunna
Ibrahiim I.S. al-Hajiri	Hawajir
Sa'd M.S.A. al-Rumayh	Sunna
Adil K.S.B. al-Subayh	SSR, Sunna
Abd al-Muhsin M.A. al-Wahayb	Sunna
Muhammad Y.A. al-Adasani	Merchant, Sunna

* speaker of Parliament (1981)

Name of Candidate	Affiliation

District VIII

Abd Allah F.A. al-Nafisi	SSR
Ahmad A.A. al-Rab'i	L
Abd Allah J.A.J. Isma'il	Shia
Ahmad F.S. al-Tukhaym	Shia
Isma'il A.A. S. Ma'rifi	Shia
Turki A.A.T.H. al-Turki	SSR
Khalid Y.A. al-Mudif	Sunna
Salah M.I.M. al-Muzaydi	Shia
Abd al-Rahman S. al-Duwaysan	Awazim
Abd al-Rahman M.A. al-Qahtani	Qahtan
Abd al-Azziz J.M.A. al-Qahtan	Qahtan
Abd al-Azziz S.A. al-Mutawi'	Merchant, Sunna
Fahd H.H. al-Siba'i	al-Siba'
Fahd A.H.D. al-Azmi	Awazim
Muhammad A.A.I. al-Hajiri	Hawajir
Muhammad A.M.I. al-Awadi	Shia
Yahiya F.A. al-Smayt	Merchant, Sunna
Ya'qub Y.M. al-Da'ij	Sunna

District IX

Jasir K.A. al-Rajihi	L
Ahmad M. al-Khatib	L, Sunna
Khalid S.S. al-Fadil	Sunna
Sa'd A. al-Salim	Sunna
Sa'id A.A. al-Uthman	Sunna
Isa M.S. al-Shahiin	IIC
Fahd K.A. al-Zamani	

District X

Sami A.A. al-Munayis	L
Salih Y.S. al-Fadalah	Merchant, Sunna
Ahmad J.S. al-Slayti	Sunna
Jassim M.S. al-Majdali	Sunna
Habiib I. Sa'ban	Shia
Abd al-Rahman A.A. al-As'usi	Merchant
Farid M. al-Ajil	SRH, Sunna
Muhammad S.A.A.A. al-Musawi	CN, Shia
Ya'qub Y.S. al-Da'ij	Sunna
Yusif A.M.S. al-Ghanim	Merchant, Sunna

Name of Candidate	Affiliation
District XI	
Muhammad S.M.A. al-Murshid	Sunna
Ahmad A.J. al-Sa'dun	Merchant, Sunna
Khalaf H.J.S. al-Tamimi	Sunna
Zayd A.S. al-Shatti	Sunna
Abd al-Latiif M. al-Banjis	Sunna
Muhammad S.M. al-Muhayni	L
Yusif S.A. al-Hussayniyah	Sunna
District XII	
Rashid A.M. al-Juwaysiri	Sunna
Salim A.H. al-Hammad	Shia
Thunayan A.T.S. al-Udhaynah	Sunna
Jam'an M.N. al-Hrayt	Utaybahi
Sa'd R.S.A. al-Azmi	Awazim
Subhi A.A.A. al-Azmi	Awazim
Ali I.M.A. Hassan	Sunna
Murdi A. Radi al-Udhaynah	Sunna
Ya'qub Y.I. al-Ali	Shia
District XIII	
Nasir A.A.H. Sarkhawa	SSC, Shia
Abbas H.S. al-Khadari	Shia
Ibrahiim A.Y. Khanbit	CN, Shia
Ibrahiim M.A. al-Maylim	Shia
Isma'il A.H. Dashti	Shia
Baqir Asad A. Asad Allah	Shia
Jamal A.J. Muhammad	SSR, Sunna
Khalid N. al-Wasmi	Awazim
Abd al-Azziz M. al-Yassin	Shia
Abd al-Latiif A.A. Farhan	Sunni
Fadil A.A.A. al-Fahd	Sunni
District XIV	
Nasir F.M. al-Banay	L, Sunna
Hamud N.A. al-Jabri	Utaybah
Ahmad Gh. M.S. al-Utaybi	Utaybah
Khalid A. al-Fahd	L
Khalid A.K. M. al-Sani'	Sunna
Salim A.S.F. al-Baghayli	Utaybah
Abd al-Razzaq A. al-Sani'	Sunna
Muhammad A.F. al-Usaymi	Sunna
Muhammad M.M. al-Rafdi	

210

Name of Candidate	Affiliation

District XV

Muhammad M.A.M. al-Musaylim	Rashaydah
Abbas H.M. al-Musaylim	Rashaydah
Ibrahiim K. al-Zamil	Mutayr
Halaywi R.Y. al-Baghayli	Utaybah
Hamud A.M. Al Daghbas	Utaybah
Khalid N.R. al-Mu'sib	Rashaydah
Salim S.R.R. al-Rashidi	al-Rashaydah
Saud I.A.K. al-Rashidi	al-Rashaydah
Shafi D.F. al-Mutayri	Mutayr
Shabib I. al-Daghbas	Utaybah
Sunaytan A.S.H. al-Diham	Utaybah
Ali S.H.B. al-Hayfi	Rashaydah
Fayiz H.B.A. al-Rashidi	Rashaydah
Falah s. al-Namran	Utaybah
Muhammad R.M.R. al-Rajihi	
Muhammad F.F. Jifidan	SSR, Rashaydah
Muhammad M.M. al-Ajmi	Ajman
Nasir M.M. al-Sayir	Utaybah
Nasir M.M. al-Zu'bi	

District XVI

Mubarak F.A.F. al-Dwaylah	SSR, Utaybah
Barrak N.F.A. Abu Qhata	Sunna
Ahmad A.A.A. Haydar	Shia
Hammad A.S.M. al-Jatayli	Aniza
Sabah M.S. al-Adwani	Adwan
Abd al-Razzaq Sh.K. al-Sharifi	
Abd al-Azziz K. al-Mukhlid	Sunna
Ubayd J.U. Farhan	
Ali H.A. al-Mulla	
Ghanim A.H.A. al-Mutayri	Mutayr
Muhammad H.N. al-Barrak	Sunna
Nayif A.A. al-Mutayri	Mutayr

Name of Candidate	Affiliation

District XVII

Yusif K.A. al-Mutayri	Mutayr, L
Faysal B.W. al-Dawish	Mutayr, L
Khalid A.U.A. al-Mutayri	Mutayr
Abd al-Kariim H. al-Jahaydali	Mutayr
Fahd S.A. al-Arnada	Rashaydah, Sunna
Mubarak F.M. al-Nout	Mutayr, Sunna
Muhammad K.D. Ashal	
Nashi A.M.M. al-Adwani	Adwan

District XVIII

Khalid D.A.J. al-Anizi	Aniza
Sayyah S.S. al-Shaybah	Utaybah
Hammad S.M.J. al-Harshani	Aniza
Khalid H. al-Haydar	Shia
Khalid S.F.A. al-Anizi	Aniza
Raja S.R.H. al-Azmi	Awazim
Ayid F.B.A. al-Shammani	Shammar
Abd Allah A.S.A. al-Badhaali	Aniza
Muhammad A.M.A. al-Ghadban	Sunna
Hudayan M.H. al-Harshani	Aniza

District XIX

Munayzil J.F. al-Anizi	Aniza
Ahmad N.M. al-Shay'an	Dafiir
Zayd R.T.F. al-Mutayri	Mutayr
Sa'di M.A. al-Dafiiri	Dafiir
Tarad A.A. al-Aniza	Aniza
Mishan M.N.S. al-Azmi	Awazim
Mutlaq S.M.A. al-Mutayri	Mutayr
Mutlaq M.S. al-Shalimi	
Mutlaq M.M. al-Saud	
Nasir I.M.A. al-Azmi	Awazim

Name of Candidate	Affiliation

DISTRICT XX

Falah M. al-Hajraf	Ajman *
Yusif M.A.S. al-Anizi	Aniza
Mufrij K.M. al-Khalifah	
Ali F.D.A. al-Shammari	Shammar
Talal U.M. al-Sa'id	Ajman
Mukhlif H.M.M. al-Jad'an	Mutayr
Azziz M.K. al-Jayb	Dafiir
Numan M.G. al-Fadli	Dafiir
Ghali J.A. al-Zayidi	Ajman
Ja'id J.K. al-Harbi	Harb
Abir U.M. al-Badhaali	Sulluba
Khali M.A. al-Ajmi	Ajman
Mubarak W.H. al-Salili	Mutayr
Sa'd N.Q.J. al-Mutawtah	Aniza
Abd Allah M.H.M. al-Sa'idi	Dafiir
Ayid S.A.A. al-Anizi	Aniza
Mubarak S. al-Walid	Mutayr
Falah Mubarak al-Hajraf	Ajman
Ali A.K. al-Sa'id	

*   Second winner not available

DISTRICT XXI

Da'yj Kh. T.M. al-Jari	Awazim
Khalid A.H. al-Ajran	Ajman
Khalid M.A. al-Najjar	Hadaar-Sunna
Rashid A.A.N. al-Azmi	Awazim
Salman M.A. al-Haqqan	
Abd Allah S.A.R. al-Ajmi	Ajman
Falih M.N. al-Mutayri	Mutayr

Name of Candidate	Affiliation
DISTRICT XXII	
Hadi H.A. al-Ajmi	Ajman
Sa'd F.T.F. al-Ajmi	Ajman
Rashid B.Q. al-Azmi	Awazim
Za'd D.A. al-Rashid	Rashaydah
Sultan S.S. al-Ajmi	Ajman
Marzuq F.A.A. al-Azmi	Awazim
Muraykhan S.S. al-Ajmi	Ajman
Muzyid A.M. al-Mutayri	Mutayr
Multi Z.H. al-Dayhani	
Nahar B.N.A. al-Mutayri	Mutayr
DISTRICT XXIII	
Mubarak F.R.R. al-Fahma'	Awazim
Khamis T.K. 'Iqab	Awazim
Sa'd B.A. al-Sa'd	Ajman
Ali A. Kh. al-Ayban	Ajman
Mansur N.F.S. al-Ajmi	Ajman
DISTRICT XXIV	
Mubarak H.H. al-Zawir	Mutayr
Rashid S.R. al-Hajaylan	Awazim
Fahd M.M. al-Azmi	Awazim
Fayhan D.A. al-Utaybi	Utaybah
Mubarak A.A. al-Dabus	Ajman
DISTRICT XXV	
Hadi S.H. al-Jalawi	Awazim
Ayid A. Kh. al-Azmi	Awazim
Abd Allah R.A.J. al-Hijri	Hajir
Thamir J.M.J.A. al-Ajmi	Ajman

Twenty-four of the fifty members of the 1981 Parliament could be identified as belonging to eight tribes. See Table 6.5 for a list of the tribes along with the number of deputies each had in the 1981 Parliament.

REFERENCES CITED

Abu Dhur 1980. *Thawha fi rihab Macca*: *haqiqat al-nidham al-Saudi*. Manshourat dar al-Tali'a.

Abu Jaber, Kamel S. 1969. The Legislature of the Hashemite Kingdom of Jordan: Study In Political Development. *The Muslim World* 59(1):220-250.

al-Ghazali, Sa'ad 1985. *Al-hayat al-dimogratiyah fi al-Kuwait*. Kuwait: National Union of Kuwaiti Students.

al-Nafisi, Abdullah F. 1978. *Al-Kuwait*: *al-Ra'd akhan*. London: Taha Advertising.

al-Sa'dun, Jasim 1984. *Manakah al-azmah wa azmat al-manakh*. Kuwait: Sharikat al-rubay'an.

Aronoff, Myron J. 1985. An Interpretation of Israeli Political Culture. Paper delivered at the American Anthropological Association's Annual Meeting, Washington.

Asiri, Ali, Kamal al-Manufi 1986. Al-intikhabat al-niyabiyah al-sadisah (1985) fi al-Kuwait tahliil siyasi. *Journal of the Social Sciences* 14(1):95-138. Kuwait: Kuwait University.

Azawi, Abbas 1936. *'Ashayir al-iraq*. Baghdad.

Bailey, Clinton 1984. *Jordan's Palestinian Challenge 1948-1983*: *A Political History*. Boulder: Westview Press.

Beinin, Joel 1981. Formation of the Egyptian Working Class. *Merip Report* 94:17-20.

Bendix, Reinhard 1967. Tradition and Modernity Reconsidered. *Comparative Studies in Society and History* 9:297-346.

215

216

Boratav, Korkut 1981. Kemalist Economic Policies
    and Etatism. In *Ataturk: Founder of a Modern
    State*, eds. Ali Kazancigil and Ergun Ozbudun,
    pp. 165-190. London: C. Hurst & Co.

Braudel, Fernand 1980. *On History*. Chicago:
    University of Chicago Press.

Celine, K. 1985. Kuwait Living on its Nerves.
    Merip Report 130:10-12.

Clifford, James 1986. Culture on Trial: History
    versus Anthropology in the Mashpee Indian Land-
    Claims Case of 1978. Lecture, Princeton
    University.

Cohen, Abner 1965. *Arab Border-Villages in Israel: A
    Study of Continuity and Change in Social
    Organization*. Manchester: Manchester University
    Press.

Cole, Donald 1975. *Nomads of the Nomads*. Chicago:
    Aldine.

Coon, Carlton S. 1953. *Caravan: The Story of the
    Middle East*. New York: Holt.

Crystal, Jill 1985. Coalitions in Oil Monarchies;
    Patterns of State-Building in the Gulf. Paper
    delivered at the American Political Science
    Association's Annual Meeting, New Orleans.

Dawisha, Adeed 1983. Jordan and the Middle East:
    The Art of Survival. In *The Shaping of an Arab
    Statesman: Sharif Abd al-Hamid Sharaf and the Modern
    Arab World*, ed. Patrick Seale, pp. 61-75.
    London: Quartet Books.

Dekmejian, R. Hrair 1971. *Egypt Under Nasir*.
    Albany: SUNY Press.

Dickson, Harold Richard Patrick 1949. *The Arab of
    the Desert*. London: Allen and Unwin Ltd.

---. 1956. *Kuwait and its Neighbours*. London:
    Allen and Unwin Ltd.

Downs, Anthony 1957. *Economic Theory of Democracy*. New York: Harper & Row.

Eickelman, Dale, F. 1986. Royal Authority and Religious Legitimacy: Morocco's Elections, 1960-1984. In *The Frailty of Authority*, ed., Myron J. Aronoff, pp. 181-205. New Brunswick and Oxford: Transaction Books.

El-Edroos, Brigadier Syed Ali 1980. *The Hashemite Arab Army 1908-1979: An Appreciation and Analysis of Military Operations*. Amman.

Eloul, Rohn 1985. The Rise and Fall of the Bedouin List: A Study of Jewish Politics in the Arab Sector. Paper delivered at the American Anthropological Association's Meeting, Washington.

Erguder, Ustun 1969. Politics of Agricultural Taxation in Turkey, 1945-1965. Ph.D. Dissertation, Syracuse University. Turkey.

---. 1980. Politics of Agricultural Price Policy in Turkey. In *The Political Economy of Income Distribution in Turkey*, eds. Ergun Ozbudun and Aydin Ulusan, pp. 169-196. New York: Holmes & Meier.

---. 1980-81. Changing Patterns of Electoral Behavior in Turkey. *Bogazici Universitesi Dergisi (Bogazici University Journal)* 8-9:45-81.

---. 1982. *Secim Sistemleri ve Turk Demokrasisi (Electoral Systems and Turkish Democracy)*. Istanbul: Bogazici University.

Farah, Tawfic, Faisal al-Salem and Mary al-Salem. 1980. Alienation and Expatriate Labor in Kuwait. *Journal of South Asian and Middle Eastern Studies* 4(1):3-40.

Fried, Morton 1967. *The Evolution of Political Society*. New York: Random House.

Geertz, Clifford 1973. The Integrative
Revolution: Primordial Sentiments and Civil
Politics In the New States. In *Interpretation of
Culture*, pp. 225-311. New York: Basic Books.

Giddens, Anthony 1979. *Central Problems In Social
Theory*. Berkeley: University of California
Press.

Gubser, Peter 1984. *Jordan: Crossroads of Middle East
Events*. Boulder: Westview Press.

Hamza, Fuad. 1933. *Qalb Jazirat al-arab*. Ryad:
Maktabat al-nasr al-haditha.

Harris, George L. 1958. *Jordan*. New Haven:
Human Relations Area Files.

Hendriks, Burtrus 1985. Egypt's Election,
Mubarak's Bind. *Merip Report* 129:11-18.

Heper, Metin 1980. Center and Periphery in the
Ottoman Empire: With Special Reference to the
Nineteenth Century. *International Political Science
Review*.

---. 1982. State and Bureaucracy in Republican
Turkey. Paper delivered at the First
International Conference on the Comparative,
Historical and Critical Analysis of
Bureaucracy, Zurich, Switzerland.

---. n.d. Bureaucrats, Politicians and Officers
in Turkey: Dilemmas of a New Political
Paradigm. In *Modern Turkey: Continuity and
Change*, ed. Ahmet Evin, Opladen: Zeske and
Budrichs (forthcoming).

---. 1985. *The State Tradition in Turkey*.
Humberley, England: The Eathon Press.

Herzfeld, Michael 1985. *The Poetics of Manhood:
Contest and Identity in a Cretan Mountain Village*.
Princeton: Princeton University Press.

Hill, Alger G. 1973. Segregation in Kuwait. In *Social Patterns in Cities*, eds. B.D. Clark and M.B. Gleave. London: Institute of British Geographers. Special Publications No. 5.

Hijaza, Ali 1964. Kuwait: Development from a semitribal, semicolonial society to democracy and sovereignty. *American Journal of Comparative Law* 13:18-438.

Jureidini, Paul A. and R. D. McLaurin 1984. *Jordan: The Impact of Social Change on The Role of the Tribes*. Washington: Praegor.

Karpat, Kemal H. 1981. Turkish Democracy at Impasse: Ideology, Party Politics and the Third Military Intervention. *International Journal of Turkish Studies* 2:1-43.

Kelley, Stanley Jr. 1983. *Interpreting Elections*. Princeton: Princeton University Press.

Key, V. O., Jr. 1955. A Theory of Critical Elections. *Journal of Politics* 17:3-18.

Labib, Yunan 1984. The Political Parties. Part fourteen of a fourteen part series (in Arabic), Musawwar.

Layne, Linda L. 1986a *The Production and Reproduction of Bedouin Identity In Jordan*. Ph.D. Dissertation, Princeton University.

---. 1986b "Tribalism" and "Orientalism": Anthropological Approaches to the Images and Self-Images of Jordan's Bedouin. Paper prepared for delivery at the American Anthropological Association's Annual Meeting, Philadelphia.

Lipset, Seymour and Stein Rokkan 1966. Cleavage Structures, Party Systems, and Voter Alignments: An Introduction. In *Party Systems and Voter Alignments: Cross-National Perspectives*, eds., Lipset and Rokkan, pp. 1-65. New York: The Free Press.

220

Mahgoub, Muhammad A. 1977. *Al-Kuwait wa al-hijra*. Alexandria: Al-haya al-masriya al-amah lil kitab.

Mardin, Serif 1966. Opposition and Control in Turkey. *Government and Opposition* 1(3):375-388.

---. 1969. Power, Civil Society and Culture in the Ottoman Empire. *Comparative Studies in Society and History* 11(3):258-282.

---. 1972. Center-Periphery in the Ottoman Empire: A Key to Turkish Politics? *Daedalus* 102:169-190.

Markaz al-khibrah lil istisharat al-ihsaiyah. n.d. *Azmat al-manakh bayna al-haqiqa wa al-khayal*. Kuwait: Dar al-haqiqa.

Meeker, Michael E. 1984. The Great Family Aghas of Turkey: A Study of a Changing Political Culture. In *Rural Politics and Social Change in the Middle East* eds., Antoun and Harik pp. 237-267. Bloomington: Indiana University Press.

Mill, John Stuart 1962. *Considerations on Representative Government*. Chicago: Henry Regnery Company.

Moench, Richard U. 1984. Plunder on the Right. Paper presented at the SWANA Conference "Egypt: The Sadat Decade in Perspective," Binghamton, New York.

Mohsen, Safia K. 1984. Laws Without Sovereignty: the Culture of Corruption. Paper presented at the SWANA Conference "Egypt: The Sadat Decade in Perspective," Binghamton, New York.

Nuseibeh, Hazem 1983. Arab Nationalism: Decades of Innocence and Challenge. In *The Shaping of an Arab Statesman*: *Sharif Abd al-Hamid Sharif and the Modern Arab World*, ed. Patrick Seale, pp. 197-209. London: Quartet Books.

Orent, Wendy 1985.   The Transfomation of Hegemony
     in Israel.   Paper delivered at the American
     Anthropological Association's Annual Meeting,
     Washington.

Oweidi, Ahmad Saleh Suleiman 1982.   *Bedouin Justice
     In Jordan (The Customary Legal System of the Tribes
     and its Integration into the Framework of State Polity
     from 1921 Onwards*).   Ph.D. dissertation,
     University of Cambridge.

Owens, Roger 1983.   Sadat's Legacy, Mubarak's
     Dilemma: Egypt in the Arab Oil Economy.   *Merip
     Report* 117:1-27.

Ozbudun, Ergun and Frank Tachau 1975.   Social
     Change and Electoral Behavior in Turkey: Toward
     A 'Critical Realignment'?   *International Journal of
     Middle Eastern Studies* 6(4):460-480.

Ozbudun, Ergun 1979.   *Social Change and Political
     Participation in Turkey*.   Princeton: Princeton
     University Press.

Pedersen, Mogens N. 1979.   The Dynamics of
     European Party Systems: Changing Patterns of
     Electoral Volatility.   *European Journal of Political
     Research* 7(1):1-26.

Petersen, Glenn 1985.   A Cultural Analysis of the
     Ponapean Vote in the 1983 Plebiscite.   *Pacific
     Studies* 9(1):13-52.

Rosen, Lawrence 1984.   *Bargaining for Reality: The
     Construction of Social Relations in a Muslim
     Community*.   Chicago: University of Chicago
     Press.

Rosen, Lawrence 1984.   Rural Political Process and
     National Political Structure in Morocco.   In
     Rural Politics and Social Change in the Middle East,
     eds., Antoun and Harik, pp. 214-237.
     Bloomington: Indiana University Press.

Rouleau, Eric 1984a.   L'Egypte en fermentation.
     Le Monde Part I, August 21.

---. 1984b. L'Egypte en fermentation. *Le Monde* Part III, August 23.

Sahlins, Marshall D. 1968. *Tribesmen*. Englewood Cliffs, New Jersey: Prentice Hall.

Sartori, Giovanni 1978. *Parties and Party Systems*. London: Cambridge University Press.

Sayari, Sabri 1977. Political Patronage in Turkey. In *Patrons and Clients*, eds. Ernest Gellner and John Waterbury, pp. 103-114. London: Duckworth & Co. ---. 1978. The Turkish Party System in Transition. *Government and Opposition* 12(1):39-57.

Service, Elman 1975. *Origins of the State and Civilization*. New York: W.W. Norton & Co.

Stokes, Donald E. 1985. The Paradox of Campaign Appeals and Election Mandates. *Proceedings of the American Philosophical Society* 129(1):20-25.

Sunar, Ilkay and Sabri Sayari n.d. Democracy in Turkey: Problems and Prospects. In *Transition From Authoritarian Rule: Experiences in Southern Europe*, ed. Phillippe C. Schmitter (forthcoming).

Sweet, Louise E. 1964. Pirates and Polities: Arab Societies of the Persian or Arab Gulf, 18th Century. *Ethnohistory* 2(3):262-280.

---. 1965. Camel Raiding of North Arabian Bedouin: A Mechanism of Ecological Adaptation. *American Anthropologist* 67:1132-50.

Tachau, Frank 1980. Parliamentary Elites: Comparisons. In *Electoral Politics in the Middle East*, eds. Landau, Jacob M. and Ergun Ozbudun and Frank Tachau, pp. 185-202. London: Croom Helm.

Utaybi, Juhayman I.M.I.S. nd. Dawat al-ikhwan: Kayfa badat wa ila ayna tasir wa al-nasiha wa al-tahdhir fi al-wuqu fi al-khatar al-kabir wa al-nafasid wa al-talbisat fi al-madaris wa al-maahid wa al-jami'at.

Warner, W. Lloyd 1959. *The Family of God: A Symbolic Study of Christian Life in America*. New Haven: Yale University Press

Weimann, Gabriel 1984. Every Day is Election Day: Press Coverage of Pre-Election Polls. In *The Roots of Begin's Success: The 1981 Israel Elections*, eds. D. Caspi, A. Diskin, and E. Gutmann. New York: St. Martin's Press.

About the Authors

Ustun Erguder, a Ph.D. of Syracuse University, is Professor of Political Science at the Faculty of Economics and and Administrative Sciences at Bogazici University, Istanbul. He has been a Research Scholar at the Institute for Social Research of the University of Michigan, a Visiting Professor at Syracuse University, and a Senior Fulbright Scholar and Visiting Professor at the University Center at Binhamton, State University of New York. Professor Erguder has contributed to the *Journal of Public Policy* and the *Bogazici University Journal* as well as to several collected volumes, and is author of two books in Turkish.

Nicolas Gavrielides is Associate Professor of Anthropology at State University of New York at Cortland. He received his Ph.D. at Indiana University. He has been a visiting Senior Research Fellow at the Maxwell School at Syracuse University and a visiting Professor at Kuwait University. Professor Gavrielides has conducted field research in Lebanon, Greece, the Arabian Gulf, and Rwanda and has published a number of articles and is currently working on a book (co-authored with Eric Davis) on Culture, Nation Building and State Formation in Arab Oil Producing Countries.

Richard I. Hofferbert has been Professor at State University of New York at Binghamton since 1975. He recieved his Ph.D. in Political Science at Indiana University and has taught on the faculties of University of Michigan, Cornell University, and Williams College. Dr. Hofferbert is the author of several books, including *The Study of Public Policy* (1974) and *The Reach and Grasp of Policy Analysis* (1986) as well as scores of articles in professional journals. Hofferbert has been Visiting Professor at the University of Mannheim, University of Lausanne, The Free University of Berlin, and Bogazici University. His primary area of specialization is comparative policy analysis.

Linda L. Layne is a part-time lecturer in the Department of Anthropology at Princeton University. She received her Ph.D in cultural anthropology and

Near Eastern Studies at Princeton University. Dr.
Layne has done fieldwork in Jordan and Algeria and
has published articles on Jordanian female factory
workers and the use of space by the Bedouin of the
Jordan Valley, and is currently working on a book
on the Production and Reproduction of Tribal Identity in Jordan.

Richard U. Moench is Associate Professor of Anthropology at State University of New York at Binghamton where he teaches economic anthropology and
theory courses. he is a co-author with Don Peretz
and Safia Mohsen of *Islam: Legacy of the Past, Challenge for the Future* NorthRiver Press; and has published articles on Chinese in the South Pacific.
His research interest in Egypt began with a sab-
batical sojourn in 1977-78, and a return trip in
1981. Dr. Moench is currently preparing an edited
book based on a conference he organized at SUNY
Binghamton in April 1984 on "Egypt: the Sadat Decade in Perspective".

Don Peretz is Professor of Political Science and
director of the program in South West Asian and
North African Studies (SWANA) at the State University of New York at Binghamton. He is the author
of *Government and Politics of Israel, the Middle East Today*, and *The West Bank: History, Politics, Society and
Economy*.

Sammy Smooha is Professor of Sociology and Chairman of the Department of Anthropology and Sociology at Haifa University in Israel. He is the author of *Israel: Pluralism and Conflict, Social Research
on Arabs in Israel, 1948-1976* and *The Orientation and
Politicization of the Arab Minority in Israel*.